"When I first read the title of this book, I wasn't sure what to expect. But with each page I realized that not only is this book describing the kind of church I want to help build, it is describing the kind of person I want to be."

KYLE IDLEMAN
Senior Pastor of Southeast Christian
and author of *Not a Fan* and *One at a Time*

"Many Christian books give the impression that the author's life is perfect and if you read their book, yours will be too. Not this one. Carl is raw, open and challenging as he gives us practical ways to deal with our mess. Only in a community where people say "I'm bleeding too" do we experience the healing that Jesus wants us to have."

JIM BURGEN
Lead Pastor of Flatirons Community Church
and author of *No More Dragons*

"The central story of this book about literal blood-stained pews is inspiring. The damage that fake Christians have done to the mission of Jesus is too much to count. I hope that believers everywhere take Carl's challenge in this book to be open about our brokenness. If you do, you will create the community of grace and truth Jesus had in mind when he said, 'I will build my church.'"

BRIAN TOME
Lead Pastor of Crossroads Church and
host of "The Aggressive Life with Brian Tome" podcast

"I lead a ministry that partners with hundreds of churches across the country. Mosaic Christian Church is one of my absolute favorites. In this book, lead pastor Carl Kuhl shares the secret recipe of what makes

Mosaic such a special church. My hope is you will read it and help your church be more of a hospital for the broken."

DARREN KEY
CEO of Christian Financial Resources, Inc.

"If Christians were honest, we'd have to admit that long before Covid, we were wearing masks. *Blood Stained Pews* creatively and practically drives home the truth that the Church is stronger and more effective when vulnerability is seen as a value and not a weakness. We reflect Christ when we welcome the wounded and at times even shed a little of our own blood on the seats of our churches."

DAVE STONE
Former Pastor of Southeast Christian Church

"It's evident that Carl knows first-hand the power of loving others through the mess. *Blood Stained Pews* calls us to a courageous choice—to lay down our defenses and embrace a culture of vulnerability that allows us to be loved more deeply than ever before and meet our once-silent struggles with the healing power of Jesus. The passion, conviction, and direction embedded in these pages won't let you turn back to the way it was."

CHARITY BYERS
Ph.D., CEO and Psychologist, Blessing Ranch Ministries
and co-author of *Unhindered* and *Unhindered Thirty Days*

"What do you think of when you think of church? Raw? Authentic? Safe? Healing? Overflowing with grace? The odds are high that you and some of the people you love have rarely experienced any of those qualities. Carl Kuhl is on a mission to change that. He will inspire you, like he has me, through the soul refreshing words of *Blood Stained Pews*, which are modeled every day by the unique and refreshing church he leads."

GENE APPEL
Senior Pastor of Eastside Christian Church, Anaheim, CA

"Carl Kuhl has written a disarmingly honest and hopeful book about how everything changes when we encounter God's grace. I've been a friend of Carl's and of Mosaic Church for years now, and can tell you that *Blood Stained Pews* isn't based on theory. God is working through Carl and Mosaic to be a living example of how those of us who feel like we are too broken or too far gone, can be redeemed and used by God. If you struggle to believe this kind of grace is for you, read this book! You might just find yourself falling in love with a God who's madly in love with you."

CHUCK MINGO
Teaching Pastor of Crossroads Church
and CEO & Founder of Courageous Love

"Carl writes with the kind of conviction that only comes from ongoing testing and refinement. He leads by example, never asking of anyone else what he isn't willing to do first. This book is a clear call for followers of Jesus, and the church at large, to be authentic, vulnerable, genuine. Carl makes a compelling case that doing so is the only way for us to experience abundant life and for the church to fulfill its God-given mission."

BRENT STORMS
President/CEO of Orchard Group

"I have long believed that it's only when we're real that Jesus can truly help us. Vulnerability is the key to wholeness. This needed book is a call to all Christians to be brutally honest, because if we can't bring our pain, questions, and shame to Jesus, why pretend that we need him at all? Jesus had the answers for the most broken people while he walked the earth. And the fakers just never got it, as a matter of fact, they killed him because they never got it. This book will help you take practical steps to be open about your brokenness, so the churches everywhere can have blood-stained pews."

TIM HARLOW
Senior Pastor of Parkview Christian Church
and author of *What Made Jesus Mad?*

BLOOD STAINED PEWS

CARL KUHL

HOW VULNERABILITY TRANSFORMS A BROKEN CHURCH INTO A CHURCH FOR THE BROKEN

Fedd Books
P.O. Box 341973
Austin, TX 78734
www.thefeddagency.com

Published in association with The Fedd Agency, Inc., a literary agency.

ISBN: 978-1-949784-90-9

eISBN: 978-1-949784-91-6

Library of Congress Number: 2021923211

Printed in the United States of America

WHAT WOULD IT TAKE FOR CHURCH TO BECOME KNOWN AS A PLACE WHERE GRACE IS "ON TAP"?

—PHILIP YANCEY

CONTENTS

INTRODUCTION

It's June 5, 1944. Nazi Germany has overtaken Europe. Poland has fallen. France has been overrun. Britain is hanging on to its freedom by a thread. The next twenty-four hours will determine the fate of Britain, Hitler, and the entirety of the Western world.

At approximately 9:30 p.m., the 101st Airborne, known as "the tip of the spear," takes off from England for Normandy on the eve of the greatest invasion in history: Operation Overlord. We know it simply as D-Day.

Two American medics, Kenneth Moore and Robert Wright, are among the nearly thirteen thousand paratroopers who are dropped into France under the cover of darkness.[1] Like most paratroopers, they miss their drop zone. Like most medics, they get separated from their supplies. The only tools they have to care for the wounded are scant items they carry strapped to their bodies.

They land at 3:00 a.m. near a small French village called Angoville-au-Plain. At first, all is quiet. But very quickly Germans and Americans spot each other, and gunfire breaks out. Moore would later say, "There's no substitute for hearing a bullet snap past your head and you realize somebody's trying to kill you."[2]

Angoville fluctuates between American and German control over the next thirty-six hours. But Moore and Wright are not there to fight the enemy—their training and purpose are to care for the wounded. As

Robert Wright sizes up the situation, he spots an old church and decides it is the perfect place to bring the wounded.

The church building itself is 900 years old.[3] It is very plain—a simple structure built of stone, with a handful of wooden pews. Wright affixes a flag with a red cross on it to the front of the door so everyone will know they are there to help. Then he and Moore get to work.

Moore finds an old farm cart that he uses to comb the village-turned-battlefield. He loads injured soldiers one at a time onto the cart and wheels them to the church. There, he lays them on pews so he and Wright can assess and treat their wounds.

At various points throughout the day, Wright and Moore's work is interrupted. At one point a German soldier bursts through the church doors, pointing his machine gun at the Americans. But when he sees them treating injured soldiers, he crosses himself in reverence and departs. Later, three German officers walk in. When they see that Moore and Wright are treating everyone, regardless of what uniform they wear, the officers promise to get a doctor on site to help as soon as possible. At one point, a bomb crashes through the ceiling and cracks the stone floor where it lands. Seconds tick by—and nothing happens. The bomb is a dud. Moore grabs it and throws it out the window, just in case.

By 10:30 p.m. on D-Day the church is packed with the wounded. All the stained glass has been destroyed by bullets.

About thirty-six hours after the 101st Airborne first landed, the fighting moves on from that area, and so do the medics. By the time they leave their makeshift aid station, Moore and Wright have treated over eighty soldiers and civilians in the church, several of them German and one of them a young local girl. Both men were awarded the Silver Star for their service in Angoville. Wright received three Purple Hearts for what he did in the war.[4]

If you go to the village of Angoville today, the church is still there.

But there is something unique about it. After the war ended, the villagers were cleaning up, trying to get back to normal. When they entered the church, they saw that blood from the soldiers Moore and Wright treated covered the wooden pews.

But the people of Angoville didn't replace the soiled pews with new, shiny ones. They didn't sand them down to make them look fresh and clean. They didn't put cushions on the pews so you wouldn't see the blood. They preserved them—with the blood still on the pews.

They wanted to make absolutely clear to future generations: this church was built in the 1100s to be a place of hope and healing for broken, hurting people, and on June 6, 1944, that's exactly what it was. It was a place for the wounded to come, for the injured to bleed, for people to be healed, for the hurting to be cared for—no matter who they were, their beliefs, or their background.

They preserved the stains to remind all who would come after: this is the church of the blood-stained pews. This is the place where the hurting can come. This is the place where the wounded can heal. This is the place where the suffering are welcome.

I visited the church in Angoville not too long ago. I saw the restored stained glass windows. I viewed the memorial to Kenneth Moore and Robert Wright. I observed the crack in the stone floor where the dud bomb had landed.

And then I saw them—the blood-stained pews. I froze, overcome with emotion. Not because I am a history buff. Not because I have an affection for old churches. Not because I have a relative who was a part of D-Day.

Seeing those blood-stained pews reminded me: this is what church is supposed to be. The church—as in, the global church—should be a place where the hurting, the broken, and the bleeding can come to get help without condemnation.

No matter the circumstance, church is the place where the outcasts and the broken can come to get help. And when people who are injured come in, they bleed. It's messy. It's gross. Sometimes it's offensive. So, while blood-stained pews are not exactly pretty—they are the necessary byproduct of a church on mission with Jesus.

The problem is, that's not true of most people's experience with church. Most people have a negative view of and negative experience with church. And when I use the word "church," please understand that I'm not talking simply about a Sunday service—I'm talking about everything that makes up the community that is the church, the body of Christ.

In his book *What's So Amazing About Grace?*, Philip Yancey wrote about a friend of his who was a social worker. The friend counseled a prostitute who was seeking help to escape her lifestyle. The woman initially sold her body to support her drug habit. Then she got into more expensive drugs, which led to her renting out her two-year-old daughter to men interested in weird sex. She was distraught, asking what to do. Finally, Yancey's friend asked, "Did you ever think of going to church for help?" She stopped short and said, "Church? Why would I ever go there? I was already feeling terrible about myself. They'd just make me feel worse." Through this shocking and heartbreaking story, Yancey points out that the very people who run *away* from the church today are those who ran *to* Jesus in the Scriptures.[5]

There are too many churches with clean pews, metaphorically speaking. And it's not that people aren't injured and bleeding; it's that we have taught them: "Don't show that wound. Cover it up so you don't bleed on others. Deal with it on your own. Pretend everything's okay." So, people stay away. And if they do come, they hide their wounds.

Although some will disagree, I believe what the church has missed in recent years is not the substance of its beliefs. I know there are exceptions, but for the most part the church as a whole does a good job standing on God's Word as truth. What the church continues to miss is the environment they build around those beliefs. A church of blood-stained pews needs to create a culture of vulnerability. In other words, this kind of church must be a people open about our brokenness, doubt, pain, anger, dreams, fears, and desires. We must acknowledge, "I'm bleeding."

I studied the history of Christianity in college. Much of it is lost on me now, but I do remember the Restoration Movement. What struck me is that its mission is not simply to reform what was already broken but to restore what was originally intended. I like that. I believe the new restoration movement will not be about theory, church authority, or sacraments. It will be about practice, grace, and community. When I first heard the story of the blood-stained pews, I thought, *This is the best image of church I've ever seen.* Isn't church supposed to be the place where the broken can bleed? Isn't it supposed to be the place where the wounded can come? Isn't the church supposed to be a hospital for the hurting? Isn't the church designed for the sinner? Didn't Jesus say, "Healthy people don't need a doctor—sick people do. I have come to call not those who think they are righteous, but those who know they are sinners" (Mark 2:17)?

Jesus was constantly reaching out to the outcasts, the broken, the rejected, the embezzlers, the sinners, the sex workers, the possessed, the injured, and the bleeding. His mission looked radically different than the priorities of the religious leaders in his day. I love Eugene Peterson's paraphrase of Jesus' words in Matthew 11:28–30 (MSG):

> Are you tired? Worn out? Burned out on religion? Come
> to me. Get away with me and you'll recover your life.
> I'll show you how to take a real rest. Walk with me and

work with me—watch how I do it. Learn the unforced rhythms of grace. I won't lay anything heavy or ill-fitting on you. Keep company with me and you'll learn to live freely and lightly.

This is who Jesus came for: the openly broken.

The reality is, bleeding people sit in the seats next to us, whether we admit it or not. If the church reaches average people, then in any given church in America:

- 1 in 4 people abuse alcohol regularly.[6]
- 1 in 4 women have had an abortion.[7]
- 1 in 20 are contemplating suicide.[8]
- 1 in 6 are actively battling anxiety disorders.[9]
- 1 in 5 men and 1 in 8 women have had or are actively having affairs.[10]

And think about this: Jesus appeals to the most broken of the broken. If hitting rock bottom is what makes people realize they need Jesus, those stats are probably *higher* in the church than anywhere else. So, why does it seem the church is not a safe place to bleed?

The church was not started to prevent pain and bloodshed. It was started to seek out those who are bleeding, bring them into the church with all their mess, and do whatever it takes to help them experience life—like Moore and Wright did on that fateful day.

We could focus all day on how the idea of church has been polluted, but we need to trace the path to its pure source and figure out together what Jesus intended the church to be. How did he interact with broken people like us? How does Jesus intend his followers to act? What does that look like in community? My ultimate goal is for you to choose vulnerability and experience the freedom that comes from the gospel colliding with your brokenness. My hope is that out of a choice to be radically vulnerable, *you* will be the change—*you* will be the impetus to create a community of openly broken people.

Recently, I felt compelled to write Yancey a letter inspired by the story I read about the social worker and the prostitute.

Dear Mr. Yancey,

Nearly twenty years ago your book *What's So Amazing About Grace?* rocked my world. I had grown up in a great church, I had accepted that grace, and I had been living in that grace. But your book took it to a depth I felt but had never heard articulated.

When I read the story of the drug-addicted mom who rented out her daughter for sex but refused to go to church for help, I had two immediate thoughts: First, I thought, if she had come to the church I grew up at, she would've found grace. But that was closely followed by this thought: not enough places have churches like that.

I was in college at the time, and I knew I had to get this message out. That ultimately led to our family moving to Maryland in 2008 to launch a new church. We knew no one in the state, so to say it was daunting is an understatement.

You wrote another book a couple years ago, *Vanishing Grace*, in which you lamented the lack of grace you have seen and how the church has not grown in its grace since your original book on grace released.

I beg to differ, and my evidence is the people who make up my church:

- A friend of mine recently shared that in the last two years, he hasn't gone four straight days without either looking at porn or having sex with someone. Many churches would kick him out. He serves on our cleaning team and attends every week.

- I have a gay friend who wakes up every day asking the same question: "God, am I an abomination?" Sometimes he thinks, "Yes, I am," and pursues hookups with other men. We have lunch every so often to talk about grace and God's ultimate truth about him.

- I pastor a woman who came to church, got baptized, got clean, and was making wise decisions. But when her man got out of prison, she got pregnant again and was making poor choices. I reached out to her and could hear the shame in her voice when she said she couldn't come to church these days. I told her, "No, this is where you *need* to be." Now, she's back and trying to figure things out.

- I have a friend who's watching his wife die of cancer. And he's been *so* faithful to Jesus. But now his question is, "Carl, how does God's grace get me through this?"

- A friend of mine is trying to move on from being a prostitute. She attends every week, compliments my sermons, and is trying to figure out if Jesus can keep her clean and away from dangerous men.

I love these people. They are screw-ups, they're outcasts, and they're broken. They keep messing up: They're just like me. Sometimes it seems we take two steps forward and three steps back.

But at the end of the day, we come together because we know we have grace. We don't really use the term "grace"—we call it "endless second chances," because we never outgrow our need for it. Grace is so hard, because how much you appreciate it is in direct proportion to how much you realize you are screwed up.

There are things I wish our church did better, but one thing I know we get right is grace: no matter who you are, where you've come from, how old you are, what religious background you have, how many people you've slept with, what race you are, how many people you've taken advantage of—our community is a place where grace is kept on tap, and the bar is always open.

Don't give up. There is hope for the church.

— Carl Kuhl

For those of you who feel cynical about the church, I get it. But the message I sent in that letter is what I want you to hear as well: don't give up. There is hope. Remember, Jesus said he came not for the healthy, but for the sick. In other words, he came to find those who'd been mortally wounded, and then he started his church as a place to bring them and heal them.

Whether you are someone who loves Jesus, but not the church, or a pastor looking to transform your church; whether you are bleeding because of your own mistakes or because of someone else's; whether you are hanging on for dear life or ready to run after those who are dying—this book is for you. This book is for you if you think Jesus is safe but his followers are not. This book is for you if the Christian community you've experienced falls short, but you know there has to be something better. This book is for you if you want to join me on the journey of rediscovering what Jesus had in mind when he started the church. It is my prayer that this journey will result in a rededication to the mission Jesus gave us. Through posturing our hearts toward vulnerability, practicing vulnerability in our communities, and realizing the power of vulnerability beyond our church doors, I believe we will look more like the church Jesus intended and experience the freedom that type of community brings.

Not long after I sent that letter to Philip Yancey, I was surprised to receive a note in return. He expressed appreciation for the kind words, and then added, "I'm sure you know that what you describe is not the norm in the average church. But it gives me hope that the gospel is still transforming lives, step by step, and God's love is being felt by us ragamuffins."

That phrase stuck with me: "What you describe is not the norm in the average church." I keep Yancey's reply framed at my desk, forcing myself to stare at that sentence as I write. That phrase is the reason for this book. People need a place where they can bleed. People need a place where they can be broken. People need a community of endless second chances. And it's not just "people" in a generic sense—I need it, and so do you.

PART 1
LOOK
INWARD

CHAPTER 1

LOOK IN THE MIRROR

IF THE BIGGEST SINNER YOU KNOW ISN'T YOU, THEN YOU DON'T
KNOW YOURSELF VERY WELL.

—JEAN LARROUX

During World War II, Andras Tamas is drafted into the army in his
native Hungary and captured by the enemy. But when he's processed,
they mistake his native Hungarian language for the gibberish of a lunatic. So, they have him committed to a Russian psychiatric hospital. Then
they forget about him—for 53 years.

However, around the year 2000, a psychiatrist at the hospital real-
izes Tamas is not, in fact, a lunatic and helps him begin to recover the
memories of who he is and where he came from. Tamas is then released
and returns home to Budapest as a war hero, dubbed "the last prisoner
of World War II."

The most peculiar part of his story is that not only has he forgotten
his real name, but he also hasn't seen his own face in five decades. A news
account shared that when they gave him a mirror, he studied his face as

though looking at it for the first time: "For hours, the old man studies the face in a mirror. The deep-set eyes. The gray stubble on the chin. The furrows of the brow. It is his face, but to him it is a startling revelation."[11]

I believe we need to follow Tamas's example and take a long look in the mirror.

Our souls desire to live in a community of open brokenness—a community of blood-stained pews—where the broken and hurting are genuinely cared for, accepted, cherished, and valued no matter what. But it requires something of us. It sounds nice to say we want a community where people are vulnerable, where hypocrisy is renounced, where we can be fully known and fully loved by God and each other. It sounds great until we realize that to experience this, we have to participate.

Vulnerability is terrifying. Admitting brokenness, weaknesses, temptations, hopes, dreams, and failures is difficult and scary. We naturally avoid being vulnerable with others in most situations, and we avoid being honest with ourselves about our own brokenness. But the first step of living in a community with blood-stained pews is being honest with ourselves—honest about how we are broken, honest that we are bleeding, honest that we need help. Because if we aren't honest, how can we expect anyone else to be?

To look inward as we pursue vulnerability, we need to acknowledge that grace is a journey, we'll never "arrive," and nothing we can do on our own can fix our brokenness. There are typically four human responses toward encountering our own brokenness:

- Pride: we justify our brokenness
- Shame: we take on the identity of our brokenness
- Apathy: we blame circumstances or others for our brokenness
- Doubt: we don't believe God can heal our brokenness

A journey that never ends...

In all these scenarios, we center ourselves and our identity on our brokenness or lack thereof rather than centering our lives on God and our identity on who he created us to be. So, the first way we change the narrative of our brokenness is this: we've got to look in the mirror.

When I think of the idea of church being a safe place for broken people to experience healing, I immediately think about the ways we convince ourselves we are the exception. I think about how everyone, in one area of their life or another, has a case of the wells. When we make excuses, it's often preceded by the word "well." For example: My wife will ask if I picked up the item she needs at the grocery and I respond, "Well, I had a stressful day, so I forgot." I ask a friend why he didn't meet me at the gym, and he says, "Well, my alarm didn't go off." I ask my kid why he was rude to his brother, and he tells me, "Well, he did it first."

It's one thing to do that for a grocery list or being late to the gym, but we do this for much more serious things as well.

- We say people shouldn't look at porn, but when we look, we think, *Well, you don't know how bad the sex is in my marriage and how stressed I am.*
- We think people should be generous, but when we leave a small tip, we rationalize, "Well, that was terrible service!"
- We think others should take a day off every week, but when we check our email on Saturday, we think, *Well, God knows my heart; it's not like I'm a workaholic.*
- We want other people to be open, but when we think of being vulnerable, we make the excuse "Well, my thing is so petty; they wouldn't understand."

We are quick to judge and condemn others while letting ourselves off the hook. Psychologists call this the Fundamental Attribution Error.[12] It works like this: when something goes well in my life, I take credit for it, believing I caused it. But if something goes wrong, I blame it on outside circumstances. For example, if I lose weight, it's because I'm disciplined; if I gain weight, it's because of my genetics. If I make money in the stock market, it's because I'm so wise; if I lose money, it's because I was unlucky.

What makes the Fundamental Attribution Error even worse is the way we explain the behavior of other people. If something goes wrong, it's their fault. For example, if other people gain weight, it's because they're undisciplined, and if they lose money, it's because they're foolish. That's the Fundamental Attribution Error at work.

We are masters at the art of self-deception. And, as we know, the first step of living in a community of blood-stained pews is being honest with ourselves. But being honest with ourselves requires vulnerability. Unfortunately, the first barrier to this type of community is a friend we know all too well: his name is Pride.

It's easy to spot pride in the athlete who gets a taunting penalty. It's easy to call it out in the performer whose lyrics are self-centered. It's obvious in the politician who talks like he will single-handedly solve the world's problems. It's a little more difficult to recognize pride in our own lives.

This makes me think of a story Jesus told. Two men go to the temple to pray. One is a Pharisee: one of the religious leaders who's great at keeping the rules. The other is a tax collector: essentially a sell-out to the Roman Empire who makes more money if he rips off his fellow Jews. But here's what happens:

> The Pharisee stood by himself and prayed this
> prayer: "I thank you, God, that I am not like other

people—cheaters, sinners, adulterers. I'm certainly not like that tax collector! I fast twice a week, and I give you a tenth of my income."

But the tax collector stood at a distance and dared not even lift his eyes to heaven as he prayed. Instead, he beat his chest in sorrow, saying, "O God, be merciful to me, for I am a sinner."

And in case we miss what's going on, Jesus makes it clear: "I tell you, this sinner, not the Pharisee, returned home justified before God. For those who exalt themselves will be humbled, and those who humble themselves will be exalted" (Luke 18:10–14).

When we read about the Pharisees, we often make the mistake of hearing anything they say with a snooty, arrogant tone that's more fitting of a bad boss on a lame sitcom than any Pharisee in Jesus' day. Pharisees were experts in religious law; they were respected and feared in their communities. When I think about his prayer, I have to ask myself how many times I have prayed things like, "God, thanks that I didn't look at porn last week. God, thanks that I give way more than a tithe. God, thanks that I don't cheat people." And what do we do in the church with someone who prays this prayer? We make him an elder!

But the tax collector knows he is the worst of sinners. Remember, in Jesus' day, tax collectors are the despised sell-outs who work for their foreign occupiers. This tax collector is aware of his brokenness: he won't even look to heaven (the typical prayer posture of the day), hits himself on the chest (that's weird), and begs for mercy (that's uncommon).

The Pharisee talks about what he did and didn't do; the tax collector focuses on the selfish condition of his heart. And Jesus makes very clear: one of these guys—and *only* one of these guys—is good with

God because one of these guys—and *only* one of these guys—knows he hasn't arrived.

Have you ever been on one of those family road trips with a young kid who constantly asked, "Are we there yet?"* Parents often joke that there's a difference between a trip and a vacation. One involves young children, and one involves happiness. While there is nothing wrong with a family trip—and, in fact, it can be a memorable time of family bonding—it should never, ever be confused with a vacation.

A friend once sent me the following list, humorously denoting the differences between a trip and a vacation:

- If you are traveling by car, there is a good chance it's a trip. If you have packed one or more "throw-up bags," clearly, it's a trip. If you packed a training potty, it's not a vacation. If packing the car leads to a fight with your spouse about who has a better "system," you, my friend, are going on a trip.
- If you can't see out the back window the entire time you are driving, it's a trip. If the children have fought about where they are sitting, it's definitely a trip. If the car has a constant smell of fast food, you are on a trip.
- If you've broken out the "all we could afford to do growing up was go camping" lecture, you are officially on a trip. If no one heard you because they all have their headphones in, it's most certainly a trip.
- If you are meeting extended family and/or in-laws—please don't insult me—it's a trip.

*If you *were* this kid, text your parents and siblings to apologize. Now. Seriously, you were really annoying.

- If there is a pack-and-play in your room, you are on a trip.
- If you are in a hotel room with two double beds: trippity trip trip. If your kids go to bed at 8:00 p.m. and you have to be quiet and locked in the room with them, that's a classic trip, my friend.
- If your destination is a tent, you are so not on a vacation. I don't even know what to tell you. You are not *even* on a trip. You are on a *camping* trip.

I love trips and I love vacations. But what this book is about is going on a journey. A journey is something entirely different from a trip. A journey is a quest. A journey may involve a battle. A journey often involves good versus evil. On a vacation I go somewhere different. On a journey I *become* someone different. On a trip my location changes; on a journey my *soul* changes.

In Jesus' story, the tax collector realized following God is a journey, that he would never arrive—whatever that would mean—and that every day of his life he would be completely in need of God's grace. But the Pharisee thought spiritual growth was a trip, and he'd arrived at the destination. Because of this, he was full of pride. The Pharisee was comparing himself to other people. That will result in pride every time and keep us from dealing with the things behind the actions that need to be dealt with.

I'm part of a spiritual formation group. This group is made up of seven men who get together most Mondays to do some soul work. One week involved exposing the lies we tell ourselves. The leader paired us up. We looked at the man across from us, with whom we'd already been in this group for many months. And the leader told us to think of a negative judgment of that man, something like, "You're a bad dad," "You're a passive husband," or "You're a lazy employee." Then, while maintaining eye contact with the other man, we had to say this judgment aloud. (Talk about uncomfortable!)

Then the facilitator asked, "What kind of man is a . . .? Fill in the blank." What kind of man is a bad dad? What kind of man is a lazy employee? We had to look the man in the eye and say the answer to that question: "You are a man who cares only about himself. You are a man who hasn't dealt with your issues."

So, we were completely uncomfortable in this exercise, wondering what in the world we were doing. And what the leader did next surprised me. He took out a mirror, had the man across from me hold it so I could see myself, then directed, "Say it again." I looked in the mirror and said the same things. In that moment, the lesson hit me like a ton of bricks: I go through life making up stories about other people based on limited data. But the reality is, the majority of the time those stories are a way for me to deflect attention from my own issues. Through those stories, I'm trying to say, "I'm not bleeding. You are!"

The truth is, I don't want the attention on me. I want to be the exception. And maybe I'm not actually those things—maybe I'm not lazy or selfish. But that's what I fear becoming in the moments when I cast condemnation on others. In other words, when I cast judgments on others, it's a clue that I'm not being real with myself about something.

See, the Pharisee in Jesus' story was consumed with the guy praying next to him, when he needed to look in the mirror and take stock of his own stuff. Sure, he didn't have the same sins as someone else, but there was some other stuff he didn't dig into because he was too busy comparing.

Dealing with our pride is vital to this idea of blood-stained pews, the idea of living freely and lightly, the idea of living with open brokenness.

The apostle Paul understood this well. He wrote thirteen books of the New Testament, started many churches, and carried the title of "apostle"—he was kind of a big deal. In a letter to Timothy, though, he calls himself the worst of sinners. What's interesting is his exact language. He doesn't say, "I *was* the worst of sinners." He says, "I *am* the worst" (1 Timothy 1:15).

"Am," as in present tense, not something he used to be. The "worst of sinners" is something he continues to be, even as he builds churches and spreads the gospel. Maybe he continues to screw up royally. Maybe as you get closer to God in your relationship with him, the darkness and depth of your sin are more noticeable. Either way, he says, "I *am* the worst."

If vulnerability leads to freedom and the first barrier to vulnerability is my pride, how do I *not* be like the Pharisee? How do I become like Paul instead? The answer is simply to reject a common line of thinking that exists today: "I need to forgive myself."

There is a lot of talk these days about self-forgiveness; it's huge in the secular world. This lie has even found its way into Christian thinking because it *sounds* right. It *sounds* like it's spiritual and grace filled. But the idea that you need to, or even can, forgive yourself is a lie from the pit of hell.

Let me explain. You will hear Christians say, "I just can't forgive myself," or, "I know God has forgiven me, but I'm struggling to forgive myself." This is the wrong mindset because forgiveness always has a cost.

Let's say that you have a cabin in the Rocky Mountains, and you say, "Carl, I know you like to ski, so why don't you use my place for free?"* So, I stay at your place and have a great time. But as I'm leaving, I back into your mailbox, run it over, and destroy it. One of two things can happen: You can decide *not* to forgive me, in which case I'm buying you a new mailbox. Or you can forgive me, but then *you* have to buy a new mailbox. Either way, *someone* is buying a new mailbox. Someone is paying the cost.

---

*Just speaking hypothetically, but you can reach me via social media. I promise to clean up after my stay.

Forgiveness *always* has a cost. Sometimes people ask, "Why did Jesus have to die on the cross?" This is why! Because *someone* had to pay for our sin. We can or he can, and he chose to do it.

Think about this with relationships. If someone wounds you deeply, to *not* forgive them means they pay the cost, meaning they no longer have a relationship with you. On the other hand, if you forgive them, you pay the cost of having to show them grace, overlook the offense, and choose to have a relationship even though it's difficult. Someone always carries the cost of forgiveness.

Let's say I've messed up. If God forgives me, he says he will take my sin. But what would it look like to forgive myself? If I'm trying to forgive myself, I'm trying to transfer the cost of this from myself to myself. So, I'm still stuck with it! But if God forgives me, I put it on him, and he pays the cost. He's taken it away; I don't have to forgive myself because the burden is gone. The beauty of the cross is that you don't have to forgive yourself, because that's what Jesus did when he died for you: "For our sake he made him to be sin who knew no sin, so that in him we might become the righteousness of God" (2 Corinthians 5:21 ESV).

When you hear people say, or even catch yourself saying, "I just want to forgive myself, but I can't"—that's correct! You *can't* forgive yourself! Grace means it's impossible to forgive myself. Satan wants you to believe you need to do something in addition to what Jesus has done for you. Scripture says Satan schemes. One way he schemes is this lie he's planted in our world that says, "I need to forgive myself." No, you don't. You can't! You just need to come to grips with the fact that Jesus has forgiven you, set you free, and made you new. He has forgiven even that thing you want to carry guilt for.

Here's why this matters: If I have to forgive myself, that's pretty daunting. I think I'll just change my perspective; I'll get a case of the wells so I'm not really that bad of a sinner. I'll lie to myself about it, and

I won't have much to forgive. But if Jesus forgives me, if it is impossible for me to forgive myself, if endless second chances are real and Jesus is the only one who offers them—then I can be honest with myself about who I am, what I do, and the things I desire.

We cannot save ourselves. We cannot achieve right standing with God. We cannot excuse our own brokenness. And we cannot forgive ourselves. Only Jesus can do those things. Like Paul and the tax collector, we must recognize we are the worst of sinners. We are on a journey of grace, we haven't arrived, and we won't arrive in this life. But through the gift of vulnerability, we get to humbly journey with others who are in the same boat.

Jesus says, "Those who exalt themselves will be humbled and those who humble themselves will be exalted" (Matthew 23:12). Being openly broken means not trying to minimize your brokenness but seeing it for what it is. It means humbly acknowledging that you cannot achieve righteousness on your own. You cannot justify yourself. You cannot forgive yourself. You need the grace and forgiveness Jesus offers.

It's hard to set aside our pride and take an honest look in the mirror. But when we do, we don't just see the darkness in our souls and the sin in our desires. We see the grace of Jesus, which means we've overcome the first barrier to being vulnerable, and we're ready to continue the journey.

CHAPTER 2
SLUMPED SHOULDERS

SHAME IS SO FRIGHTFUL TO MAN THAT IT IS ONE OF THE
INGREDIENTS OF HELL ITSELF ...

—CHARLES SPURGEON

"I dare you to preach a sermon that's not all about *you*."

My feet were glued to the floor as I stared this stranger in the face, receiving her unsolicited feedback. It was Christmas Eve, packed crowds filled the building during this event, and there was a buzz in the air that only happens with the magic of Christmas. After each service, I stood in our lobby to say hi to people, pray with those who needed prayer, and wish people a "Merry Christmas."

Over the course of several services, I had gotten compliment after compliment about my sermon; how funny it was, how insightful it was, how helpful it was. But then I met *her*—my self-appointed sermon critic. She introduced herself, then explained that she doesn't go to church but attends ours every Christmas. Then she dropped the bomb she really wanted to share: "Every Christmas I come here, and you always just talk about yourself—it's very off-putting to new people, you know."

I was so taken aback I literally laughed out loud and said, "Merry Christmas!" Then, with a look of malice she tried to disguise as wisdom, she said, "I dare you one Christmas to preach a sermon that's not all about you!" and she walked off.*

Here's the thing, I had gotten probably twenty compliments on my message prior to Ms. Sermon Critic. But do you know what feedback I was stewing over the rest of the day? That's right: hers. I started to think, *Maybe she's right. Maybe this is all about me. Maybe I'm an arrogant jerk who doesn't represent Jesus well. Maybe I should never preach on Christmas again. Maybe I shouldn't preach anywhere ever again. Maybe I should open a landscaping business so I don't have to get that kind of feedback. I mean, if you plant flowers in the wrong place, people won't personally attack you, right?*

But as I thought about it more, I realized a couple of things. First, what people get out of a sermon message has more to do with their hearts than my sermon. Those people who said the message was great—well, it was because they walked into church wanting to hear from God, so they did. But that woman listened with a cynical heart, so she also heard what she wanted to hear.

Still, that didn't explain why it bothered me so much. After some soul searching, I realized the honest answer is: because I wanted it to. I had unintentionally positioned my soul to receive all the feedback as if it was about *me*, not about *them*. Every time a person said, "Good message," "Thanks for the sermon," or "That really impacted me," I had chosen to receive it as if it was about me, to think that I was such a good speaker that *I* had impacted them.

Therefore, when someone came up who was cynical, I had already

---

*I think we can all agree she got coal in her stocking the next day.

made the decision that whatever they said was about me, not them; so when she gave me the critique, I had to carry the weight of that in my soul. I had decided to put my self-worth in the hands of other people. I had decided to live in a way that what I did is who I am. I had chosen the path of shame.

SHAME RESPONSE

"Shame" has become a buzzword in our world, and I believe that is a helpful thing. Genesis tells us that when Adam and Eve entered the world, they were naked and "felt *no shame*" (2:25, emphasis mine). Think about that: God created us to live without shame. Shame is the result of sin. It's real. It's powerful. The *only* thing we know Adam and Eve felt after sin entered the world is shame (see Genesis 3:7). Shame is the defining feeling of a life separated from God. Our shame drives us from God, and being away from God makes us feel shame. It's a dangerous cycle.

In her TED talk on shame, Dr. Brené Brown said, "Shame drives two big tapes: 'never good enough' and … 'Who do you think you are?'" She says shame is correlated with things like "addiction, depression, violence, aggression, bullying, suicide, and eating disorders." Shame is an epidemic in our culture.[13]

The best way I know to diagnose shame is this: shame is when I feel small.

It's when your mom makes a comment about your parenting, but emotionally you go to the ways she manipulated you when you were a kid, and everything in you wants to unload on her. It's when a boss or teacher corrects you and did so in a healthy way, but you associate being corrected with not being good enough, and you're on the edge of a panic attack. It's when you look at the money coming in and the bills that are due, and they don't line up and you don't just think, *This is a challenge*; instead, you think, *I'm not a man, because a real man would provide for his family*. It's when your girlfriend wants to have a DTR, but your emotions go back to when you got the "mom and dad don't love each other anymore" speech, and you want to run and hide. It's when you mess up as a parent—again—and you just *know* your kids are screwed. It's when you talk with your ex and she says that one phrase or gives you that one look—and it still feels like she owns you.

You feel small.

And shame is a big reason why we don't want to be vulnerable, right? We don't want to admit this stuff. Most of the time, our shame sounds ridiculous to verbalize. Because shame is brought on by simple things like upsizing our French fries, messing up our makeup, or our sports team losing; it just sounds ridiculous, so we stuff it. The problem is, when we stuff our shame about the ways we are broken and bleeding, we miss out on the freedom and grace God freely offers us, and we miss out on our shame becoming part of our ongoing story of redemption. When shame infiltrates our narrative of brokenness, it insists that the ways we are messed up are part of our identity—fundamental to who we are.[14]

It's vital that we see how Jesus treats shame. And that leads us to Peter. Peter was one of the men in Jesus' inner circle, he had seen Jesus perform miracle after miracle, he traveled with Jesus, and he had dropped everything in his life to follow Jesus.

Hours before Jesus is arrested, he eats dinner with his disciples and says, "I tell you the truth, Peter—before the rooster crows tomorrow morning, you will deny three times that you even know me" (John 13:38). Peter of course denies this could happen. But once Jesus is arrested, that's exactly what happens. Peter is in the courtyard outside of where Jesus is on trial. First, someone recognizes him as one of Jesus' followers, but he denies it. Then someone else says the same thing; again he denies it. Then about an hour later someone recognizes Peter's accent and says, "You've got to be with Jesus, because he talks the same way!"

(Matthew 26:73, author's paraphrase).* And Peter again denies it. In fact, he basically says, "God can damn me to hell if I know Jesus!" (see v. 74).

Here's the worst part in my opinion. Right after the third denial, Scripture says, "At that moment the Lord turned and looked at Peter" (Luke 22:61). I think this has to be the low point for Jesus. I've read that crucifixion is the worst death a human can suffer. But to know one of your best friends denies even knowing you, to hear that one of the very people you're dying for doesn't want anything to do with you—I think this is the low point.

But I also have to wonder, what did Peter feel? We know what he *did*: he "left the courtyard, weeping bitterly" (Luke 22:62). Peter came face to face with his brokenness. He had failed, and he let it define him. I believe he felt shame. Maybe the more Peter dwelled on his shame, the more he took on the identity of his actions. Maybe he didn't merely think he had screwed up but thought he *was* a screw-up.

We face the same choice Peter did. When we mess up, we can go one of two places: guilt or shame. And it's important to understand the differences between the two.

Shame is about who I am. Guilt is about what I did.
Guilt says, "I didn't treat that person with respect."
Shame says, "I'm a horrible person."
Guilt says, "I sinned against God."
Shame says, "I'll never be who God wants me to be."

*I could've told Peter that your accent can do you in. One time when we had first moved to Maryland, a friend brought a guest up to meet me after I had just preached. She looked at me with her head cocked, skepticism in her eyes, and she asked me, "Where are you from?" I said, "Kentucky." She said, "Yeah you are." I don't know what she meant, but she's never been back!

Shame keeps you stuck; guilt moves you forward.
When you experience shame, you don't want to deal
with it. So, if you feel shame about being overweight, you
might feel stuck and decide not to go to the gym. But if
you realize you're guilty of not taking care of your body,
you go deal with it. Guilt is feeling bad about something
and can inspire us to act differently in the future.

Shame is about me. Guilt is about others. I snap at my
wife because I feel ashamed that she may think I don't
know what I'm doing. It's about me. But guilt is about
others: "How did I hurt you? I want to make that right.
How did I ignore you? I want to serve you."

Shame causes pain. Guilt holds accountable. Shame
is about making someone feel unworthy, different, or
less than me.[15] Shameful comments are meant to hurt.
Comments that create guilty feelings are about communicating pain or disappointment and hoping for restoration, without communicating anything about the
person as a whole.

You're probably thinking, *Wow, guilt sounds great! How do I live
that way?* How do we transition from a response of shame to guilt? It all
comes down to understanding our identity.

IDENTITY SHIFT

Like many Christians my age, I was faithfully taught a method of evan-
gelism growing up called Romans Road.* The idea is, you can explain the

---

*You are also a Christian my age if you listened to ska music, attended overnight
lock-ins, wore a WWJD bracelet, or kissed dating goodbye.

entire gospel message using only a handful of verses from the book of Romans. And while I love the idea of explaining the gospel in a simple way, there is a serious omission in that methodology.

The first verse of Romans Road says this: "For everyone has sinned; we all fall short of God's glorious standard" (Romans 3:23). Let me translate that for you: the first step in telling someone about the "good news" of Jesus is "You're going to hell because you're pure evil!" That doesn't sound like very good news.

And listen, I get that we are sinners. I believe that! However, if that is the first truth of Christianity, in an effort to be "good Christians," many of us start believing we should do nothing but beat ourselves up over how pathetic we are, what losers we are, how we can never do anything right.

While I *am* a sinner, that is *not* the foundational truth about me. For that, we need to go to the first chapter of the Bible. When God creates the universe, he creates humankind as the crown of his creation. He creates man in his image, and then the Scripture says something that it does not say about any other part of creation. It says God looked on his creation and saw it was "*very* good" (Genesis 1:31, emphasis mine). Catch this: it wasn't *very* good before humans entered the picture. It was just good.

Created the sun. Good.
Created fish. Good.
Created cows so we could have filet mignon. Good.
Created dogs so we could have man's best friend. Good.
Created cats, for some unknown reason? Good.
Created humans. **Very** good.

You were created with intentionality, purpose, and worth. *This* is the foundational truth of the Scriptures. After that, *then* we can get to: "you're a sinner who falls short of God's standard." But it's important to remember that "sinner" is not the principal truth about you: "created" is.

Shame is a popular topic these days. I've listened to podcasts, watched TED talks, and read books on shame and vulnerability—they're obviously hitting a felt need. And I've benefited from these resources. Heck, I quote many of them in this book.

But there's a key difference in how the world talks about shame and how the New Testament combats shame. The message of these books and podcasts is: "You're worthy. Shame can't define you. You're enough just as you are." And while I agree, I don't understand their reasoning. Without the gospel, those authors and speakers are basically telling me to muster up enough self-confidence on my own to believe I'm worthy.

But the person who follows Jesus does not have to manufacture self-confidence. Rather, we know the foundational truth of our existence is that God created us with purpose and worth. The gospel, then, teaches me that *God* makes me worthy, *Jesus* makes me enough, the *Holy Spirit* helps me not live in the past. Without the gospel, culture's message on shame is to just do your best to put it aside. The gospel message is that Jesus takes it away.

Because the foundational truth of my existence is that I was formed by the loving Creator of the universe with intentionality and care, then I can come to grips with my brokenness, honestly seeing it for all it is because there's probably still hope for me. *That* is why I can be vulnerable. *That* is why I can be open about my brokenness.

WHEN SHAME MEETS GRACE

Fortunately, Peter's story doesn't end in shame. After Jesus is crucified and rises from the grave, Peter hears of this, sees the empty tomb, and then goes back to his old job of being a fisherman. So, Jesus seeks him out. And if you know the story, you know Jesus asks three times, "Peter, do you love me?" One question for each time Peter denied him. And Peter basically gets annoyed by Jesus asking this. He says, "Of course I do!" And Jesus says, "Then feed my sheep," which is an allusion to the task Jesus has for Peter: beginning the church (see John 21).

Jesus communicated, "Peter, I've got grace for you." Once Peter's shame encountered Jesus' grace, he was freed from the burden of his failure. It no longer defined who he was. And the same thing can happen for us.

But there's another part of the story where we need to connect the dots. Peter's denial is recorded in *every* Gospel. All four of Jesus' biographers include it. Those biographies were copied and spread everywhere that Christians lived. They were the good news, after all. *Everyone* knew this story. And when you think about it, the only reason it could've been written down is if it was known before it was written down. I can't emphasize this enough: *everyone* knew Peter had denied Jesus.

And when Jesus is on trial, that looks bad. But it looks *really* bad after Jesus has risen from the grave. I imagine the conversations went something like this:

> "Wait a minute, Peter; you're the one who denied you
> even knew Jesus?"
> Yep.
> "The same Jesus who rose from the grave, proving
> he's God?"
> Same one.
> "You said you never even knew him."
> That's right.
> "Three times?"
> Three times.
> "You even said God should send you to hell if you know
> Jesus. Wow, Peter, that's pretty messed up."
> I know. That's why I follow him. I need him.

Please, please catch this. It was Peter's biggest failure that enabled him to be the church's biggest catalyst. On Pentecost Sunday, when people from different nations had gathered in Jerusalem and the Holy Spirit had been given to the believers, the person who then stands up and explains who Jesus is, is the person who has the most scandalous story of denying who Jesus is. And I can't say for sure, but I think one of the reasons people listened to Peter is they knew: if *this* guy can get grace, maybe there's hope for me.

————————————

The night Jesus was arrested, not one but two disciples betrayed him. And their stories display the two ways we handle shame. We can let it drive us to Jesus and then live in Christian community, like Peter. Or we can be Judas.

Judas is the one who, for thirty pieces of silver, leads the opponents to Jesus so they can arrest him. But after Jesus is arrested, Judas feels shame. He gives the money back, but his shame doesn't go away. He doesn't know what to do with his shame, so he hangs himself.

See, the difference between guilt and shame is the difference between repentance and remorse.

Shame results in remorse. Guilt results in repentance. Remorse leads to shame. Repentance leads to freedom. One is a cycle of self-loathing. One is a path to healing.

You know the only person in Scripture who's identified as having remorse? That's right: Judas. Remorse plays the shame loop tape that says, "I have to fix this myself." That was impossible for Judas to do, so he took what he thought was his only way out.

When faced with your sin, your brokenness, will you choose the path of repentance or that of remorse? We're told to repent when we come to Jesus, and to repent means to change your mind and go the other direction. Remorse simply means to feel bad, to have regret. One leads to sorrow; one leads to change. One leads to shame; one leads to guilt. One leads to destruction; one leads to freedom in Jesus.

––––––––––––––––––

It's worth asking ourselves some questions: Is there something in my past that's still holding me captive? Is there an area where shame and remorse have power over me? Because of Jesus, I can repent, it stays in my past, and I can move on. I need to change that remorse to repentance. I probably need to talk to another Christian about that. I may even need to go to a therapist to figure out how to let Jesus unchain me from this so I can walk in freedom.

When my son London was young and would get in trouble, he had a habit that reminds me of what we're talking about. If he disobeyed his mom—say she told him to pick up his toys and he didn't—I'd call him in and correct him. But as soon as I started correcting him, his shoulders slumped, his head lowered a little bit, and he put his hands over his eyes. He didn't want to look in my eyes. He didn't want me to see him. So, I'd pull his hands down, make him look me in the eye, and I'd tell him, "London, your daddy loves you. But you can't do that." And not every time, but when he understood what I was saying, he'd straighten back up, smile, and say, "Yes, sir." Then, he would go on playing.

A lot of Christians are walking around with our shoulders slumped. There are too many Christians sitting in pews with their shoulders slumped. While they may not physically place their hands over their eyes, they definitely have their hands over their soul because they feel ashamed. Because someone told you that broken part of you is who you are: That infertility—that's who you are. That financial debt you carry— that's who you are. That time you got that girl pregnant—that's who you are. That lousy parenting—that's who you are. That allegation—that's who you are.

You have your own issues. There may be root issues from how you were raised or traumatic experiences you've had. But it comes down to this one main question: *Do I believe God?*

You have shame about being single. Do you really believe God cares about you and that if he wants you to be married will send you somebody, and if he doesn't, it will still be okay? You have shame about how your kids turned out. Do you really believe God offers grace, or are their decisions the final verdict on who you are? You have shame about your addiction. Do you really believe God uses imperfect people, or are you doomed to a cycle of failures? You have shame about your career. Do you really believe God cares more about the character of your person than the title on your business card?

What I want you to understand is that in a church of blood-stained pews, Jesus puts hands on your shoulders. He says, "Look me in the eye. That's not who you are. Because your Dad loves you, and I died for you, even if you do that thing again, I'll still see you the same way."

When you look inward and all you can see is the shame that drags you down and tells you lies about who you are, don't run and hide. Instead, bring that shame to Jesus. Let him speak into your identity. Repent and turn to him. In bringing your shame to Jesus, you will always be met with grace that takes away your shame.

Shame loves to hide in darkness, but in repenting and bringing it to the light, you will find purpose in your brokenness as God begins redeeming your story. By being openly broken, even in the areas where you feel the most shame, you are opening yourself up to healing in ways you never thought possible.

CHAPTER 3

YOU HAVE HAD A HEART ATTACK

ABOVE ALL, DO NOT LIE TO YOURSELF.

—FYODOR DOSTOYEVSKY

Have you ever visited one of those websites that helps you self-diagnose what medical problem you have?* A while back, I had some weird pain, so I went to one of those sites where you answer different triage questions. I kept clicking the different yes/no options until finally it gave me my diagnosis, along with a message that said, "You have had a heart attack. Call an ambulance immediately."

I did *not* call an ambulance. I was young, in marathon shape, and just had some weird pain. Instead of doing what the website said, I went back to the browser and changed a few answers, until I came up with

---

*It's a fun activity if you're bored. I even saw an article recently called "How to Diagnose People You Don't Like with Personality Disorders." Good times.

a diagnosis that I liked.* That's only funny because I was *not* having a heart attack.

The problem is that we do the same thing to disguise legitimate emotional and spiritual problems, and it's killing us.

Another natural response that we have toward our own brokenness is apathy. We convince ourselves that there's nothing we can do about our brokenness, and we choose to become victims of our circumstances. We refuse to make any change that could free us or heal us.

Recently, someone accurately pointed out to me the difference between being victimized and being a victim. Being victimized is something that is done to you against your will. Living as a victim is a choice you make. This really made me think about the ways we like to change the narrative in our lives, choosing to be victims in our brokenness.

When we grow apathetic in our approach to healing, eventually we become comfortable in our brokenness; we then shut God out from certain parts of our lives. But he wants to redeem and restore us fully. Part of pursuing vulnerability is asking ourselves where apathy has convinced us we are victims of our circumstances and that pursuing healing would be pointless.

The Gospel of John shows us that Jesus is aware of the ways apathy keeps us from pursuing healing from our brokenness. At the beginning of chapter 5, Jesus is at the pool of Bethesda (vv. 1–9), where there is a weird tradition that when the water bubbles up, an angel is touching it, and whatever sick person enters the pool first will be healed. So, this pool is surrounded by sick people, day after day, just watching for the bubbles.

You might think Jesus would just go around zapping everyone at this

---

*I think the recommended treatment was something along the lines of "Eat junk food and nap until you feel better."

pool with his supernatural Jesus-healing powers to restore them all. But Jesus knows nothing really changes on the most important level if a person's mindset doesn't change. So, Jesus doesn't perform a mass healing at Bethesda. Instead, he begins talking to a guy who has been unable to walk for thirty-eight years. This man probably has a family member or friend who drops him off every morning, and all day every day he begs for a few coins to buy bread to eat.

But I love what Jesus does. Jesus doesn't heal the man immediately but asks him a question: "Would you like to get well?" (v. 6). On the surface, it seems like a pointless question—he's at the healing pool, isn't he? The reality is that Jesus' question doesn't just seem pointless; it sounds insensitive. It feels mean. We might think, *Jesus, what right do you have to ask someone who hasn't been able to walk for thirty-eight freaking years if they want to get well?*

But maybe Jesus is challenging this man's victim mindset: "Are you going to choose to be a victim, blame your circumstances, and be apathetic toward your healing, or will you take action to do something about your illness?"

When Jesus asks if he wants to get well, the man responds: "I can't ... I have no one to put me in the pool" (v. 7). As in, "It's not my fault I can't get well. I'm a victim; I have no choice." In other words, "Lay off, Jesus. I'm doing the best I can with what I've got." And the guy is crippled, so I understand his annoyance. However, I hear myself in his words too because I say the same things: "I'm a victim. I'm trying. Lay off, Jesus. This is the best I've got."

In some ways, we're just like this man. Staring down on our brokenness can be overwhelming. Rather than acknowledging our brokenness, taking responsibility, and looking to God for healing, we take on the identity of victim. Then, we neglect our responsibility and sit there day after day, crippled by a mindset that says, "It's not my fault."

Do you want to get well? A lot of us would *say* we want the full and satisfying life that Jesus promises and that we want to be part of a church of blood-stained pews. Here's the thing, though: it's easy to sit on a pew. The question is, will we just take up space, or will we bleed? Will we try to get in the pool or stay on the outskirts? Are we willing to be open about our brokenness and to the opportunity for healing?

Ultimately, we have to ask, are we going to believe the lies we tell ourselves? The man in the story disguised his apathy by choosing to believe he was a victim. What's the lie you tell yourself? We all have them. The biggest lie I choose to believe is "I've given my best effort." But it's actually stronger than that: the biggest lie I *enjoy* believing is that I've given my best effort. It's where I'm most apathetic about my brokenness. It can be with working out, writing, healthy eating, parenting, pursuing purity, stretching myself intellectually, showing kindness to a stranger, you name it. I *love* convincing myself that I gave my best.

I'm good at rationalizing why the effort I gave was 100 percent. I try to tell myself this lie all the time, because if I can convince myself I gave my all, then I don't have to carry the weight of any negative consequences. After all, it was the best I could do. Right?

But it's a lie. Very rarely do I honestly give the full 100 percent effort I'm capable of. Giving 100 percent is exhausting. It's hard. It's not fun. It's easier to browse YouTube, check social media, or sit on the couch. So, I choose to be lazy, and then I choose to lie to myself about it. In fact, the lie I tell myself is the same lie the guy in our story tells: "I'm doing the best I can."

I must recognize this tendency to lie to myself and continually confess it to God. I wish he'd take away this desire to exaggerate my effort, because honestly it sounds pathetic. He hasn't yet. So, I find myself confessing over and over to God that I didn't give my all, and—once again—it cost me.

Now, I get that for some people, apathy toward being vulnerable with other Christians is born out of past pain. And I want to acknowledge that some people have experienced so much hurt that they would rather sit in that pain than vulnerably put themselves in a position where they could be hurt again.

I think of a friend of mine who worked in a church for years before I knew her. Her church once tried to build a bigger building and their financial goal was ambitious. So, they essentially locked their staff in a room and said, "To meet our goal you have to give this amount, and we're not leaving until you've done that." By the time they left, my friend had taken off her engagement diamond and put it in the middle of the table because it was the only valuable thing she owned. After years of seeing the power struggles, arrogance, and manipulation from the leaders of that church, she said, "I'm out," and she got a job in real estate.

I think of a high school buddy of mine named Paul. Paul was always unique; he wanted to be different and live on the edge. But when he went to a small Christian liberal arts college, he was told, "You can't do that. You can't think this. Don't ask that." He felt like the personality God gave him wasn't good enough for the Christians he was around, so he said, "I'm out." Paul hasn't been in church in years and doesn't pursue God at all.

And I also think of my friend who grew up in a Catholic neighborhood in New Jersey, where he was the only Jewish kid. The other kids in the neighborhood would tease him and chant, "You're going to hell! You're going to hell." Although they were just kids, that's all he needed. He won't talk about Jesus.

You could probably go through your contact list and find people you know who say they've been burned by God, Christians, or the church. And they've walked away because no matter how inviting Jesus was, his followers did not reflect that.

In the early years of the church we planted, we met in a movie theater; so every week as you walked into church, you saw on the marquee the movie that would be playing right after church above the Theater 19 door. One week the marquee displayed the title *Drag Me to Hell*. I laughed at what people would see as they walked into church, but then I realized that's what a lot of people attending a church service think is about to happen to them, isn't it?

Although the number of people who label themselves "irreligious" continues to climb, most people in our country have been heavily involved in church at some point. Maybe it was involvement in a high school youth group, the cool Christian campus ministry, or maybe mom dragged them to church growing up. The point is that most people know the deal. They know the basic message is that God loves you, sent Jesus to redeem you, and offers grace. But something happened along the way where they left. They chose apathy in their brokenness because it was better than opening themselves up to be hurt again. I know dealing with our apathy is a risk, because apathy is often a defense mechanism to keep us from being burned or hurt again.

If you've been victimized, I want you to hear this: it is not your fault. I am sad with you that people or institutions took advantage of you or hurt you. But let me remind you what is on the other side of dealing with your apathy: it's the same thing for you as it was for the man in our story—healing, and, through that, freedom. When you choose to face the lies you've believed and be vulnerable, only then can you experience the healing and live in the freedom Jesus offers.

"Would you like to get well?" is maybe Jesus' most penetrating question ever. He challenges this man to look inward and says, "Look at yourself honestly. Look at your situation. How did you get here? What are you going to do about it?"

Eventually, Jesus says to the man at the pool, "Stand up, pick up your mat, and walk!" (v. 8). And look at what happens: "Instantly, the man was healed! He rolled up his sleeping mat and began walking!" (v. 9). I love that Jesus heals him, yet the man still has to act. Think about that for a minute. Think about the vulnerability and trust the man shows by standing up. In that moment, he doesn't make any excuses or dwell on his victimhood; he acts. We can't meet Jesus halfway to holiness; rather, we need to walk toward him to accept the grace he freely offers. We act to show our faith, not to prove our righteousness. That's how it always works.*

When we see our brokenness and decide to push the blame, sit in the pain, and consider ourselves victims of our circumstance—when we choose to remain in our brokenness rather than take action to change— we are distorting the narrative of our brokenness so it's not about us. And we are not opening ourselves fully to be transformed by God's healing and grace.

Like the man who had been crippled for thirty-eight years, sometimes we feel that it is impossible to escape our brokenness, so we just live with it and consider it part of us. We take the posture of self-pity, and in doing so, we give ourselves permission to continue bleeding while we stand outside the church doors, going on and on about how we wish we were well. If we want to be a church of blood-stained pews, we need to identify any apathy in our hearts and take action toward healing. We need to stand up from our mats and start walking.

———

After the birth of our second child, I hit a wall. My wife, Lindsay, and I

---

*Jesus always asks that people *show* their faith: "Go, show yourself to the priest" (Luke 5:14, NIV). "Pick up your mat, and walk" (John 5:8). "Go wash yourself in the pool of Siloam" (John 9:7). "Anyone who believes and is baptized will be saved" (Mark 16:16).

had two kids under two years old, meaning our lives consisted of sleep-less nights and poopy diapers. We had recently moved to a state where we knew no one, meaning we didn't have deep friendships. And the church we had started was small with slow growth, meaning a lot of work with little visible payoff. In other words, life was a grind.

One day, I got home from work and sat down at the kitchen table while my kids crawled on the floor at my feet. As my wife cooked dinner, she asked about my day, and I replied with one-word answers.

"How was your day?"
"Fine."
"Did you get a lot done?"
"Sure."
"Any interesting conversations?"
"No."

This was not the first time she had experienced this numbness in my emotion. So, she paused her cooking, looked me in the eyes, and asked, "Are you okay?"

I replied numbly, "I don't know."

With tears in her eyes, she said, "Babe, you need to get help."

I didn't want to admit she was right, but out of respect for her I sought out a Christian counselor. At our first meeting, I told him about the conversation with my wife. Then I spent the next thirty minutes giving him a quick summary of my upbringing. When I concluded by explaining my current emotional indifference, he said, "Ah, you chose to harden your heart when you were a kid. We just need to help you learn how to feel."

My first thought was, *This is going to be really expensive.* But he brought me face to face with how the biggest lie I tell myself was fleshing itself out. I told you my biggest lie is that I give my best effort. In this case, I was giving effort to *doing* things: trying, working, achieving. But I gave minimal effort to dealing with my emotions, being emotionally present, and recognizing that God gave me my emotions as a gift to be used for good.

It took many months of counseling to deal with my emotional numbness. In fact, I still deal with it. I talked to my counselor about it just last week. But somewhere along the way I chose to believe a lie that I don't need to give effort to how I feel. Confronting that lie is hard. But it was as if Jesus was asking me if I wanted to get well, and I said yes. It's a process. It's not fun, but it is worthwhile. I've experienced the emotional connection with others that is only possible when you are emotionally vulnerable.

It's time to face your apathy. It's time to pursue healing. It's time to ask, "How am I lying to myself?"

- Are you lying to yourself about your marriage? You have everyone convinced it's all her fault. But deep inside, you know you don't really try.
- Are you lying to yourself about your faith? You tell other people you're mad at God, and you do a pretty good job of convincing people your situation is unfair, but you know you're twisting the facts so your anger sounds justifiable.
- Are you lying to yourself about your career? You always blame the boss, but the common denominator in all those bad jobs is you.
- Are you lying about your health? You tell other people you're trying to eat healthily, but your definition of "trying" is flexible.
- Are you lying about your pride? You talk about the questions

that keep you from Jesus, but you know deep down that the only thing keeping you from selling out to Jesus is that you simply want to be in charge.

Go to that dark place where the lie resides. Before you even think about bleeding in church community, be honest with yourself about what that dark place is. Ask yourself:

- What lie am I telling?
- Where am I choosing to be a victim?
- Where do I not want to admit I need help?

You've got to be honest, and you can start by being honest with yourself.

Jesus asks the man, "Do you want to get well?" He asks us the same question. Stop making excuses. You've changed the answers to avoid the diagnosis for long enough. It's time to be honest. Only when you're real can you attack the apathy that has crippled you.

CHAPTER 4

THE BEST PRAYER EVER

DOUBT ALWAYS COEXISTS WITH FAITH, FOR IN THE PRESENCE OF CERTAINTY WHO WOULD NEED FAITH AT ALL?

—PHILIP YANCEY

When my kids were toddlers, they did something that maybe every kid in history has done. If they saw me walking up the stairs as they were coming down the stairs, a grin would spread across their faces, they would freeze right where they were, and then they would leap into my arms. When they were very little, they would take pride in how many steps they could jump from. One step—easy. A two-step leap? Got it. Jumping from three steps? That was the skill of champions. Jumping to Dad from four steps away? Well, maybe next time.

I don't remember many of these specific jumps, but one sticks out in my mind because of how much it scared me. I was carrying some folded laundry upstairs.* These stairs turned at some weird angles. As

---

*I should note, for when my wife reads this, that I did not actually *do* the laundry… I was simply carrying it upstairs.

I rounded the last corner, I saw my three-year-old daughter, Reagan, at the top of the stairs. She loved jumping to me off the stairs, so she said, "Catch me, Daddy!"

I said, "Reagan, I can't—I have this basket of folded laundry."

I said no, but you know what my daughter did? She jumped! So you know what I did? I moved to the side and let her crash into the wall like she deserved!

Not really.

In reality, I barely hung on to the basket with one hand, I caught my daughter with the other hand—at least caught her enough so she didn't get hurt. My heart was racing because she almost fell down the stairs. I tried to scold her, explaining that no means no. But when I set Reagan down, she laughed as she skipped the rest of the way down the stairs

She ignored my warning not to jump because it never crossed her mind that her daddy would drop her. That's cute for a three-year-old. But how many of us have felt like we leaped into the arms of God and he didn't catch us? Maybe it was the prayers for a sick loved one that went unanswered. Maybe it was questions of faith that never received a good answer. Maybe it was asking for grace and still feeling weighed down in guilt.

It even seems that American Christianity has this dual personality where we talk about the #BlessedLife and Jesus working all things together for good, and at the same time, we talk about Jesus comforting the mourning and weeping with those who weep. I can defend both of those perspectives from Scripture, which makes it more difficult to help those going through a difficult time, those who cannot possibly see the good in their situation.

In our modern Christian culture, there is a pervasive attitude of "Act like everything's okay. After all, doesn't Romans 8 say God works everything together for good? So just put on a smile, be full of the joy of the Lord, and talk about how blessed you are to have hope."

I'm calling bull. That's not how it works in the real world. People who can bury a child and the next month smile as if everything's great because they're just "full of the joy of the Lord" aren't being real either with themselves or with God about their pain or the doubt their pain causes.

In his book *Disappointment with God*, Phillip Yancey shares a letter he had received from a mom of a child with cystic fibrosis. She wrote in detail about the agony of physical pain that no doctor, no medicine, no comfort from mom could alleviate. This mother watched her child die a terrible death, even as that child clung to faith in God. She ended her letter by saying,

> So, it's against this background of human beings falling apart—nurses can only stay on that floor so long because they could not do more to help—that God, who could have helped, looked down on a young woman devoted to him … and decided to sit on his hands and let her death top the horror charts of cystic fibrosis deaths.

> …it does not help to talk of the good that results from pain. Nor does it help to talk of God almost always letting the physical process of disease run its course. Because if he ever intervenes, then at every point of human suffering he makes a decision to intervene or not, and in [my child's] case his choice was to let C.F. rip. There are moments when my only responses are grief and an anger as violent as any I have ever known.[16]

Theologically, I have a hard time arguing with her statement. And emotionally, I've been to the place where we ask those hard questions. If there's one thing you're guaranteed as a pastor, it's a front row seat to pain. At the time I'm writing these words, this is what my world has been like for the last nine months:

- Two of my friends died of cancer—young.
- Another friend's kid was diagnosed with cancer—he's ten.
- Another friend with a terminal illness had an experimental medical treatment that's supposed to make him all better. It didn't work.

I'm almost to the point where I don't think I should pray for people to get well, because lately everyone I've prayed for dies. The worst of all of this was performing the funeral for my ten-year-old niece. During a funeral I try to make people laugh; it doesn't take away pain, but I believe it's cathartic. I got the mom, my sister-in-law, to laugh. I got the crowd and my wife to laugh. But I never could get the dad to laugh—I'm not sure he's laughed yet. They celebrated Easter by visiting the grave of their ten-year-old daughter.

I've visited the delivery room that should've been full of joy, and instead I ended up praying with a couple holding their dead baby boy. I've held the weeping man in my arms who says, "After years of marriage, my wife says she's gay and she's leaving me." I've done the funeral of the man in his twenties, where there weren't even that many tears because the family said, "Drugs killed our son a long time ago. The boy we knew has been dead for years."

Everywhere I look, there's pain.

When things like that happen, you experience the gamut of emotions—anger, grief, depression, the whole range. But what do you do with that when it comes to God? In my quiet moments when I'm *really* honest, I ask, "Jesus, is something wrong with me that it is hard to believe right now? Am I doing something wrong, since I don't think you're running the world very well right now?"

And before you point your theological finger at me or send me a

Bible-verse-laden email, let me reassure you: I'm still following Jesus. He is without a doubt my hope, my anchor, and my rock. Jesus never gets mad at anyone who asks him honest questions. But I just need to express where I am sometimes—some days I walk in the joy of the Lord all day long, and other days I feel like Peter when everyone else deserts Jesus and he basically says, "Where else will we go?" (see John 6:68).

But the inevitable conclusion of experiencing pain in this world is having doubt, which just becomes another reason we struggle to be vulnerable. We hold the promises of God in our hands and the pain of this world in our hearts, and we think, *How could God let this happen? Where was he when I needed him?* We don't have any answers. Our thoughts sound like borderline heresy. So, we close ourselves off and try to deal with our questions alone.

One thing I love about the New Testament is how relatable some of the disciples and followers of Jesus are. They talk with Jesus face to face, see him perform miracles, hear him teach, and yet still doubt him and his power. When my faith feels small, it's encouraging to read some of those stories and be reminded that I'm not alone in my doubts and that even small faith allows for God to move in big ways.

This is why I love the story of Jesus encountering a dad in Mark 9. A local father hears that maybe Jesus can heal his son. The son is possessed by a demon and suffers from what we'd call epilepsy. He brings his son to Jesus' disciples, but they can't heal him. So, the dad becomes frustrated. Finally, Jesus approaches and interrupts to find out what's going on.

After the dad explains, Jesus says he can heal the son if the man believes. The man responds with one of the great lines in all of Scripture. He says, "I do believe, but help me overcome my unbelief" (Mark 9:24). When you think about it, that's not showing a ton of confidence in Jesus. The dad obviously has *some* confidence, *some* faith in Jesus, because he brings his son there, but it's not exactly a ringing endorsement for Jesus as the all-powerful Creator and Redeemer of the universe.

Still, there are two beautiful things about this. One is the dad's complete honesty with Jesus. He says, "Jesus, here's where I am. I'm coming to you because I'm out of options; I don't know what else to do. I'm here because I love my kid, and I'll do anything to help him, and well, maybe you can help. But I don't believe all the way. I don't have 100 percent confidence this will work, but I do believe a little bit, so if that's enough that's what I've got." The second beautiful thing is Jesus' response. Jesus doesn't say, "You don't have enough faith, you weak-minded fool. You must have perfect faith if you want me to help you." Jesus simply heals the boy and gives him to his father.

That story should give us confidence that it's okay when we don't believe with perfect faith all the time. John Ortberg said, "Disciples are not people who never doubt. They doubt and worship. They doubt and serve. They doubt and help each other with their doubts. They doubt and practice faithfulness. They doubt and wait for their doubt one day to be turned to knowing."[17] It's okay to have questions. It's okay to doubt. It's okay to question your own belief. But we must bring that imperfect faith to Jesus. Somewhere along the line, I picked up a false belief that I should only let Jesus know about my perfect faith—the thing I really trusted him in—and if I doubted, then that was bad and therefore I should hide that. But my favorite thing about the man in this story is that he was real with Jesus, and we must be real with Jesus too.

See, we can talk all day long about how great it would be to be in a church of blood-stained pews, but if you can't be real with God, there's no way you're bleeding in front of other people. So, let's talk about three areas we need to be real with God about: disappointment, desires, and distress.

REAL ABOUT DISAPPOINTMENT

The book *Mother Teresa: Come Be My Light* is the published correspondence between Mother Teresa and her confessors and superiors over a period of sixty-six years. These letters reveal that for the last nearly half century of her life she experienced the absence of the presence of God in her life. She once wrote to a superior, "Jesus has a very special love for you. [But] as for me—the silence and the emptiness is so great—that I look and do not see,—Listen and do not hear—the tongue moves [in prayer] but does not speak . . . I want you to pray for me."[18]

She used words like "darkness" and "torture" to explain what she was feeling. She compared the experience to hell and at one point said it has driven her to doubt the existence of heaven and even of God. She was acutely aware of the discrepancy between her inner state and her public demeanor. She even wrote that "The smile is a mask ... that covers everything."[19]

The public reaction to this book and these revelations was what you would expect: atheists and Christians both felt vindicated in their beliefs.[20] I suppose you could get depressed and think, *If Mother Teresa didn't feel connected to God, what hope is there for me?* But the flipside is actually encouraging. I have complaints against God too. I feel the silence of God too. So, maybe I'm not so different from Mother Teresa after all.

I think the reason Jesus welcomes our openness is that he knows pain and disappointment too. Hebrews 4:15 says Jesus faced everything we faced. I'm not certain of the depths of what that means theologically, but I am confident it means He experienced our same emotions. After all, Jesus himself said, "Father ... let this cup of suffering be taken away from me" (Matthew 26:39) and "My God, my God, why have you abandoned me?" (Matthew 27:46). Jesus experienced anguish, anger, and deep sadness. Maybe I'm not so different from Jesus either.

A few years ago, my friend Kyle performed a funeral for a twenty-five-year-old man who had died of a drug overdose. The day the guy died, Kyle was sitting in a quiet room with the young man's mother. She was a single mom who had just lost her only child. She was a committed Christian but was very angry with God. Kyle was explaining to her that God is there with her, that she is not alone, and that when she hurts, he hurts. In the middle of his explanation—through her tears, anger, and frustration—she started a sentence: "What does God know about . . ." And she caught herself. Kyle said, "I don't know for sure what she was going to say, but I think she was going to say something along the lines of 'What does God know about losing a son?'" But she caught herself—and neither of them said anything for a long time.[21]

God knows your pain and understands your disappointment—you don't need to hide it from him and pretend you have perfect faith. Just be honest.

John chapter 11 is famous for having the shortest verse in the Bible: "Jesus wept" (v. 35, ESV). That alone is a powerful statement, but maybe equally powerful is the statement that's repeated twice earlier in this chapter. The story starts with Jesus hearing that his friend Lazarus is sick but purposefully waiting to go see him. While Jesus is waiting, Lazarus dies.

When Jesus does finally show up, each of Lazarus's sisters confronts Jesus with the same accusation: "Lord, if only you had been here, my brother would not have died" (John 11:21, 32). We can't gloss over this: They're still in the period of weeping. Lazarus died young. Jesus could've prevented this. This statement is not a simple "Jesus, you're great but one small detail to remind you of." No, this is the sisters putting their finger in Jesus' chest and saying, "This is on *you*, Jesus!"

But catch this: Jesus doesn't push back. He doesn't chastise them for their accusations. He doesn't get disappointed in their understanding. He weeps. In Jesus we see the face of God, and it's a face streaked with tears.[22] That means you can be real with God about your disappointments.

When you're mad about the abuse, tell him. When you want to scream because you're still single, tell him. When you're frustrated because the only answer to your prayers is silence, tell him. Whatever you thought was off-limits to talk to God about—tell him. He can handle it.

I once received a prayer request at church from someone who was trying to be real with God about disappointment. It said, "Help me have the honesty to admit how angry I am with God." That's the prayer of someone who's trying to be real with God about disappointment.

REAL ABOUT DESIRE

We also need to be real with God about our desires. I think this is why the psalms are in the Bible. One of the most striking is Psalm 59. It starts off simple enough: "Rescue me from my enemies . . . save me . . . I have done nothing wrong" (vv. 1, 2, 4). But it quickly turns dark: "Wake up and punish [them] . . . Show no mercy. . . . Let them be captured by their pride . . . Destroy them in your anger!" (vv. 5, 12–13).

Another one that jumps off the page is Psalm 109, which begins with David asking God to intervene with his enemies. Then he lists what his enemies are saying. Here's my paraphrase: "Count his prayers as sins. Let him die so his wife has no husband and his kids have no father. May his children wander as beggars. Let his wealth rot away so his family doesn't get it. May all his descendants die and his name be forgotten. Just curse him with the curse of all curses" (vv. 6–19). David lists all these things his enemies have said and then politely adds, "May those curses become the Lord's punishment for my accusers" (v. 20).

Don't rush too quickly past what David is doing here. Remember, the psalms were written as worship songs. So, this is the equivalent of your favorite Christian band singing a song that goes like this:

God, I know some really mean people.

God, they're saying bad things about me.

God, please don't kill them.

Instead, can you electrocute them, pluck out their eyes,

and take them just to the brink of death so they can suf-

fer before you kill them?

God, you're the best.

I love you.

Amen.

I'm guessing that wouldn't fly in this week's worship set, but that's the kind of song David sometimes sang. This makes me think we might be missing something. The example from the Scriptures isn't the example we get from Christian radio these days because the example from the Scriptures is that we bring all our desires to God, unsanitized, unedited, and uncut. Sometimes that means bringing to him desires that sound evil—things like killing our enemies, making their kids die, and them losing all their money. That sounds so wrong, doesn't it? But it's what David said.

The flipside of this is that sometimes it means bringing our desires that aren't evil but may sound selfish: "God, I want to be married. God, I want a kid. God, I want this job, God, I want to get in that college. God, I want to make the team. God, I want to travel there." Are those wrong things to ask? That's not the point. Looking back at John 11, Jesus doesn't get into a deep discussion with Lazarus's sisters about their theology in thinking he should've been there. He just weeps. In Mark 9, he didn't scold the father for not having enough belief; he just healed the boy. And he didn't strike David down for asking him to curse his enemies.

We all have longings we want to see fulfilled, but some of those dreams remain empty.

- The ring finger remains empty.
- The baby crib is still in the box, unassembled.
- The chair Grandma always sat in at Thanksgiving will be open this year.
- The inbox we check for the college acceptance letter disappoints us daily.
- Because of financial constraints, the area under the tree this Christmas will be noticeably unimpressive.

In the quiet moments of our soul that are dark to everyone else, we utter, "God, are you really there? Or should I look for something else?" Things aren't how we want them, and we've equated following God with things going right—or with not bleeding.

Please don't miss this: God is less concerned about the theological accuracy of what you say to him than he is about you sharing what is in your soul. David is called a man after God's own heart, and David is the one who asked God to kill the children of his enemies. The man with the possessed son wasn't trying to gain approval either; he was just being real. He laid it all out on the table before Jesus. Jesus never gets mad at anyone for being honest.

The man in Mark 9 understood he didn't need to be perfect to come to Jesus. Really, that's what is at the root of us putting up a front with God—the belief that we must act a certain way, say certain things, believe certain things, and if we don't, then we're out. Somewhere along the way, we picked up this belief that if we don't do those things, then we're depending on God less. But the reality is, when we are honest with God, we're depending on God more. We're basically saying: "God, *even in the pain*, I will come to you. Even in the grief, even in the loneliness, even with the addiction, even with the bipolar disorder, even with unfulfilled desires, even with the marriage that's falling apart, even with my failings as a parent, even with how I hurt people and seemingly can't stop myself—I will come to you to pray, vent, complain, and ask. I will come to you because, God, I believe you can meet me where I am and heal me, but help my unbelief."

REAL ABOUT DISTRESS

A few years ago, I hiked the Half Dome in Yosemite National Park.[23] It's a seventeen-mile roundtrip hike up and back, with 4,800 feet gain in elevation. We got up at 5:00 a.m. My backpack was so heavy with bottles of water and sports drinks that I thought I was going to tip over backward. We passed multiple waterfalls. We climbed a staircase hewn into the rock, and I just knew if you fell off you were—done. We saw the Vernal Falls up close. We spotted a baby black bear, knowing momma bear was probably close.* We saw the terrifying power of the mountain before we even reached the cables to hike the half dome itself. When we finally reached the top and gazed over the mountains and the seemingly tiny Yosemite Valley carved out by glaciers below, it was overwhelming.

But it wasn't just a cool experience—it was a spiritual experience. The day before we hiked the Half Dome, the leader of our group asked, "What is God going to teach you on that mountain?" To be honest, I was cynical about his question and my answer was something like, "Um, he's going to teach us to be careful?" But when I reached the top, gazed on the beauty of God's creation, and saw the valley that he had carved out years before, I was overwhelmed with his power.

I immediately thought of the thing that had been keeping me up at night lately, and it was like God was shaking my shoulders to take notice. I was losing sleep over a big project involving lots of money. And yet,

---

*Technically, a friend and I chased that baby black bear. When it disappeared and we rejoined the group to tell them about it, another guy asked, "Didn't you think mama bear was close?" Long pause. "Um, no, we actually didn't think about that." Whoops.

I had just completed a death-defying hike that was terrifying for this guy who's scared of heights. But as I stood at the cliff looking 4,737 feet straight down into the valley below, the lesson hit me: I realized that if God could carve this valley with a glacier at his word, my financial problems probably weren't too big for him to handle. I had an encounter with God on top of that mountain. There, I was honest about how the weight of leadership was affecting me, and it was a landmark moment of realization for me.

Honestly, I don't know if I would've been real with God if I hadn't gotten to that physical place. Mark Batterson says, "Change of pace plus change of place equals change of perspective."[24] That is so true. So, here's the question: Where can you be honest with God? A mountain? A beach? A specific chair in your house? A journal? A lonely path you like to hike? Find that place. Go to that place. And have it out with God.

I know some of you read my story of Yosemite and thought, *That's all you got? The thing keeping you up at night was simply some financial decision? Carl, I wish I had your problems!* I get it, but being real with God isn't about comparing your stuff to what someone else is going through. It's about bringing *your* stuff, whatever that is, to God. The dad in Mark 9 didn't compare his situation to other people. He brought his sick son and his doubts. What you bring will be different.

Larry Osborne shared that when he preached a sermon titled "Where's God When All Hell Breaks Loose?" they did a question-and-answer session after. The mother of a severely handicapped boy, who suffered from life-threatening seizures, initially pushed back on the idea of Larry's talk. She said God wasn't the instigator of her family's problems. She claimed it gave her purpose, meaning, and strength to see her son's condition as God's plan for her life. Then suddenly she began to sob— deep, gut-wrenching sobs. Then, she finally got honest with God as she cried out, "When will he fix this? I can't take it anymore. Why doesn't he answer?" She had finally gotten real with God.[25]

FROM THE MOUTHS OF CHILDREN

If you don't know what to say to God when you're real with him, let me help you with the words of a two-year-old. Several years ago, my niece taught me the words to say to God when I don't know what else to say. It's a simple prayer that I now consider the Best Prayer Ever. It was something that my sister used in trying to teach a two-year-old how to pray, but it has now become my go-to prayer because it so accurately and simply catches all my emotion, problems, doubts, and questions. I don't know if I've ever heard a prayer that better captures the depth of our desire for and dependence upon God. It goes like this:

> Jesus,
> Help.
> Amen.

That's it. "Jesus, help. Amen."

- I've got this marriage thing and it's driving me nuts. I can't even concentrate on what I need to do—Jesus, help.
- I'm still grieving the loss. It's been twenty-three months, and everyone said life would be back to normal, but it will never be back to normal. I don't understand why I should pray for anything ever again—Jesus, help.
- I did that same thing on the internet last night. I'm disgusted with myself—Jesus, help.
- I'm lonely. People tell me I should just rely on you, but I'll be honest, that's not good enough—Jesus, help.

Be real with God. He can handle it. He will show you grace. No one ever gets in trouble for being honest with God. Take your disappointments and desires to him. He will hear you.

Jesus, help. Amen.

Finding the healing and freedom that come from being a part of a community with blood-stained pews starts with looking inward. We can't expect others to be vulnerable if we will not be vulnerable. We can't ask people to bleed on the pews if we're standing outside the church doors covering our wounds.

Throughout the New Testament, we see people model this posture of vulnerability. Followers of Jesus look inward to address the pride, shame, apathy, and unbelief in their hearts. They lay it all out on the table before Jesus. From the tax collector who in humility admits his sin and seeks grace, to Peter who in his shame chooses to repent and turn to Jesus, to the man who hasn't been able to walk for thirty-eight years and lays his apathy aside and takes action toward healing, to the dad whose son was possessed and took a leap of faith to bring his honest doubts to Jesus.

They say, "Here is my brokenness. Jesus, help." And Jesus meets them with grace every single time.

Look inward, push your shoulders back, stand up, and walk toward God. Even and especially in the pride, shame, apathy, and doubt. This is the posture of vulnerability. We know we can trust God, so we have to take the leap. He'll be there to catch us.

As we look inward and encounter the tendencies that get in the way of us being honest about our brokenness, we can start being more open with those around us. After looking inward, it's time to embrace the awkward and begin practicing vulnerability within a community of other broken believers.

PART 2

EMBRACE THE AWKWARD

CHAPTER 5

WAX ON, WAX OFF

WHEN THE CHURCH ISN'T FOR THE SUFFERING AND BROKEN,
THEN THE CHURCH ISN'T FOR CHRIST. BECAUSE JESUS, WITH HIS
PIERCED SIDE, IS ALWAYS ON THE SIDE OF THE BROKEN.

—ANN VOSKAMP

Don't you hate awkward moments?

I know some people enjoy awkward moments for some reason, but I hate awkward moments. For instance:

- That awkward moment when you notice someone's zipper is down, but you don't want to say anything because you don't have a good excuse for why you were looking that low.
- That awkward moment when someone asks when your baby is due and you say, "Two years ago."
- That awkward moment when you see a nine-year-old with a girlfriend—and you're still single.
- That awkward moment when your eleventh birthday passes, and you get legitimately disappointed that you didn't receive an invite to Hogwarts.

- That awkward moment when you realize you had something between your teeth but none of your friends told you.
- That awkward moment when you change your status to "single" and your ex "likes" it.

I hate awkward moments. And yet, opening up in Christian community, choosing vulnerability, is awkward. In the spirit of making things just a little more awkward, I want to give you some warnings: So far, our journey of vulnerability hasn't been very awkward because it's just been internal—between us and God. But to experience what God has planned for us, that vulnerability must move beyond the internal to being expressed externally in a community of believers. I know it's hard to look inward, but it may be even harder to open up to other people; this is what I call "embracing the awkward." Before we even jump into specifics, I want to spend this chapter calling out the obvious—this is *hard*.

An Indian philosopher by the name of Bara Dada once said, "Jesus is ideal and wonderful, but you Christians—you are not like him."[26] That's a common refrain in our culture today too. We hear it most often in these words: "I like Jesus, but not the church." Based on the stories we hear in the news and in our own communities, I get it. Jesus offers grace to the broken and the hurting, but it often seems that his people want to throw stones, cast blame, and pass judgment. Many people come to church because they're bleeding, but instead of getting medical treatment, they find themselves back in the line of fire. They run to an aid station only to find another battle.

Here's the problem with saying you like Jesus but not the church: Jesus says the church is his bride. I've been married awhile now, and I still don't know everything about marriage, but one thing I do know is this: If you don't like my wife, we're not friends. If you say, "That Carl guy is pretty amazing, but his wife is just rude and selfish," I am more likely to punch you in the face than give you a warm embrace. For the record, my wife is neither of those things, but even if she were, I'd still want to punch you in the face—because she's my wife, and you don't get to talk about her that way. The point is that my wife and I are joined together, so if you don't like one of us, you're rejecting both of us.

Since the church is the bride of Christ, it seems pretty clear that you *can't* "love Jesus but hate the church," as so many people often say. In fact, I believe people know this intuitively because you don't just see people walking away from the church today; you see them walking away from Jesus. The fastest growing segment of faith in the Western world today is the "Nones," people who identify "none" on a survey of what religion they claim.[27] People are walking away from Jesus *because* they are walking away from church.

You see, when the church is good, it's great. It starts schools, helps struggling marriages, feeds the hungry, provides clean water, inspires the next generation, and on and on. But when the church is bad—it's brutal. It brushes some sin under the rug while calling out other, seemingly equal sin. It calls for purity while ignoring child abuse. It focuses on being right but neglects being relevant.

I read in the news just recently about a high-ranking church official who covered up child abuse allegations for years because he didn't want one priest to lose his job. I read about a pastor whose church forced him to quit because he had an affair; then another church hired him, only to find out he was having yet another affair, so he got fired a second time. I've talked with a woman who was told she was going to hell and wouldn't be welcomed back at her church when it became public knowledge that she was getting divorced. And those stories don't even touch the gossip, the unforgiveness, and the hypocrisy that so many of us experience in the church on a regular basis. But I don't want to spend my time arguing about who is responsible for the bad reputation the church has today. I want to rediscover what Jesus had in mind when he started his church.

The book of Acts describes the early church as being united on mission and living in community. To be clear, the early church wasn't without its drama—at one point, a married couple lies about their giving and they both fall over, dead, in front of the apostles (see Acts 5:1–11). Another time there's an argument between two ministry partners that's so intense they decide they can't even go on the same mission trip together (see Acts 15:36–40). But overall, the early church experienced exponential growth because it was an irresistible community that practiced radical generosity, overcame racial differences, and chose boldness despite opposition. As a result, it spread like wildfire. That's not what I see in the church today.

As we work toward being a church with blood-stained pews, after we look inward, we need to be vulnerable in Christian community. The way we handle our brokenness and others' brokenness will set the culture of the church. Do we want to participate in a culture where everyone feels the need to hide or get their act together before stepping into the church, or do we want to practice vulnerability in such a way that builds lasting and life-giving community with the people around us? If we want to be part of a church with blood-stained pews, we must embrace the awkward.

POTTERY LESSONS

In his letter to the Romans, Paul exhorts his audience to practice "genuine" love (Romans 12:9 ESV). This word "genuine" is interesting because the Latin word used for "genuine" in Paul's time meant "without wax," as in: love without wax.[28] What the heck does that mean?

Well, it came from a practice involving pottery. In the Roman world, people needed their pottery to drink, cook, and practice daily life. But when you make pottery, sometimes it cracks in the fire that hardens it. So, devious entrepreneurs would take some wax, put it in the cracks, then paint over it so you couldn't tell it was cracked. The result was a pot that didn't have integrity; it would break easily. If you bought a pot like this, you were getting scammed. So, when you shopped for pottery, you would look for one without wax, knowing it was sturdier. And that's why Paul says, "love without wax," meaning, "love in a genuine way."

The problem in the church is, a lot of us put wax on our cracks! We cover up the broken parts, the cracked parts, and the vulnerable parts. We try to show others that we're good, everything's fine, no need to worry about anything over here. But what we need to be, instead of first-century scam-pottery, is kintsugi pottery.

Legend has it that the ancient Japanese art form of kintsugi began in the fifteenth century when Emperor Ashikaga Yoshimasa broke a prized Chinese tea bowl given to him as a gift. He was emotionally attached to the bowl, so he was distraught. He shipped it off to China to be repaired; it was only mended with what were essentially bulky staples. That wouldn't do, so he called a Japanese craftsman to figure out how to piece it back together in a more aesthetically pleasing way.[29]

The craftsman realized there was no way to truly hide the cracks. So, he used melted gold to fuse the broken pieces together. The result was a pot that had gold highlights everywhere it had been fractured. It wasn't less desirable for having been broken; it was now more valuable because the artist used a precious metal to put it back together. And the art of kintsugi was born.[30] Today, people seek out kintsugi pottery. The pieces' flaws aren't hidden; they're highlighted. The expert artist's golden touch makes the pottery both more beautiful and more valuable.

Kintsugi is what the church is supposed to be. Church is not meant to be a place where fear and shame drive us to hide our brokenness. Rather, church is where the gold of God's grace draws attention to where He's mended us to make us whole again. It shows that we are real, demonstrates the amazing grace of Jesus for all, and displays the power of the church when it's at its best.

Like the potters, we try to deal with our brokenness in different ways.

Sometimes we try to ignore or hide brokenness, like the Roman potter. Sometimes we try to fix ourselves and others through our own wisdom, like the Chinese potter. And sometimes, like the Japanese artist, we realize we need something stronger to redeem the brokenness. When we see our flaws as opportunities for redemption rather than blemishes on our image, we become a church built on vulnerability and grace. And only then can we be the church Jesus intended.

I believe we can once again be what the church was always designed to be. I believe you can experience church where it's not just okay but encouraged to be open about your brokenness. I believe church can be a community where they don't leave you when you bleed; they help you. I believe this can be the norm. It is possible for you to be part of a church with blood-stained pews, where the broken and hurting are truly welcomed and helped every single day.

Our attempts to cover up our brokenness or try to fix it ourselves leave us weak and limit others from experiencing the grace and joy provided through vulnerability. Only through God's grace can we be made whole.

We'll spend the second part of this book figuring out how to practically be vulnerable in a community of believers. But first, let's dig deeper into why this even matters.

WAXING PHARISAIC*

We're often hesitant to be vulnerable because we're not sure Christians are safe. Sometimes it seems they're looking to catch us doing something wrong more than help us do what is right. The good news is, Jesus understands. He constantly butted heads with the Pharisees for this exact

---

*If you caught the '80s movie reference in the title of this chapter, congratulations, you also are a fan of good movies. If you didn't catch it, congratulations . . . you're younger than I am.

reason. They infuriated him when they were more concerned about legalism than helping people find God.

This is illustrated in a story in the Gospel of Mark that gives me comfort. It is one of several events that occurred on the Sabbath. The Sabbath went from sundown Friday night to sundown Saturday night, and the Jewish law required it to be a day of rest and no work. But the question for the devoted was, what counts as work? So, the religious leaders devoted countless discussions and writings to figuring out what does and does not count as work. Over the centuries they developed a list for everyone to follow. Some of these rules included:

- You couldn't walk more than 5/8 of a mile.[31]
- If you were riding a donkey and got off at dusk on the Sabbath, you couldn't take off the saddle.[32]
- You couldn't gargle vinegar if you had a sore throat because that's work.[33]
- There was a debate about whether you could eat an egg laid on the Sabbath because the chicken was working.[34]

You get the picture. Jesus was constantly butting heads with the religious leaders about the Sabbath because they were missing the heart behind God's law, focusing instead on their made-up interpretations of it. As you can imagine, this type of stuff pushed many people away from God and religious people. Broken people needed help with their everyday lives, but the things the religious leaders wanted to talk about were whether they walked six tenths of a mile or seven tenths of a mile from their houses—no thanks!

In our story, Jesus notices a man with a deformed hand. Mark tells us, "Since it was the Sabbath, Jesus' enemies watched him closely. If he healed the man's hand, they planned to accuse him of working on the

Sabbath" (3:2). (You can tell these guys are just great.) Jesus makes no attempt at being subtle. He calls the man to stand in front of them and then asks them, "'Does the law permit good deeds on the Sabbath, or is it a day for doing evil? Is this a day to save life or to destroy it?' But they wouldn't answer him" (Mark 3:4).

Then Jesus does what you would expect: Jesus heals him. It is a great miracle. This guy's life is changed forever. Imagine him going home to tell his family. Imagine how he could get back to woodworking, helping around the house, or throwing a ball with his kids. Jesus did what Jesus does—he heals the broken.

Of course, Jesus does that a lot. There's one small detail in this story that makes it more noteworthy than some others: Between Jesus' question and the man's healing, Mark gives us an insight into what Jesus is thinking and feeling, and you can probably relate. Mark tells us that Jesus "looked around at them angrily and was deeply saddened by their hard hearts" (Mark 3:5). These guys are standing in the presence of God himself and witness an amazing miracle, only to leave and plot how to kill Jesus. That's messed up.

Jesus' response comforts me. We are often sold this image of Jesus in which he's always happy, maybe even glowing. I can't relate to that Jesus. But I can relate to a Jesus who gets both mad and sad because some religious leaders care more about their own agenda than they do about people who are hurting.

Think about this: what makes Jesus mad? It's people who care more about the religious checklist than helping the hurting. What makes Jesus sad? It's people who think acknowledging brokenness gets in the way of organized religion. But what does Jesus focus on? Helping hurting people. Here's the point: Jesus feels the same way you do about the things that make you mad and sad about God, Christians, and the church. He doesn't like things that get in the way of helping hurting people either.

While I love this narrative in Mark, my favorite time that Jesus went off on the religious leaders is found in Luke 11. He's at one of the religious leaders' homes for dinner, and while everyone else goes through some ancient hand-washing ritual, Jesus just takes his seat. The host is surprised by this, so Jesus takes his cue: "Then the Lord said to him, 'You Pharisees are so careful to clean the outside of the cup and the dish, but inside you are filthy—full of greed and wickedness! Fools! Didn't God make the inside as well as the outside?'" (Luke 11:39–40).

I'm not sure how the host responded to his guest calling him filthy, greedy, wicked, and foolish. But I do wish I could see his facial expression. Whatever it was, this story makes me relate to Jesus more, because I don't care for empty religious tradition either.

As vulnerability becomes something we do in community, we need to create a culture of open brokenness, not empty tradition. By viewing vulnerability as a path to redemption, we can begin practicing openness, living in community, walking in truth, and initiating vulnerability. This will create a community where we are healed and others are drawn in to living vulnerably as well. Then we will see grace fill the gaps where we've been broken by sin.

In pursuit of a community harmoniously connected by God's grace, we need to be genuine, without wax, and we need to make sure we are not trying to fix our brokenness through our own wisdom. When we learn that we can't manufacture grace, we get closer to striking gold.

DIY SOLUTIONS

I am not what you would call a handy person, so when my wife said she wanted me to do a DIY project to put a glaze on our kitchen table, I got nervous. Like every great handyman does before a DIY project at home—I educated myself with a single YouTube video. One of the things the video taught me was, if you have cracks on the table, put painter's tape underneath the table on the cracks, so it will fill up with glaze and won't drip through. I did this and I was ready to go.

I start pouring the mixed glaze onto the table, and immediately hear an unsettling noise that sounds curiously like epoxy glaze dripping through the cracks onto the floor. I looked under the table to find that my painter's tape wasn't doing a thing. But I'm from Kentucky, so I know what can fix *all* DIY projects. I yelled to my six-year-old, "Buddy, get the duct tape—stat!" He sprinted in with the duct tape, and I got on the floor, trying to tape this up without it dripping into my eyes and mouth. After a solid taping job, I stood up to get back to the spreading part, but here's the problem: this stuff dries in about twenty seconds. So, we ended up with epoxy glaze on about 80 percent of the table.

At this point I was pretty sure I'd ruined our kitchen table (because who wants a half-glazed table), and the entire thing was a disaster. I was covered in epoxy too. Added to this was the stress of knowing that my entire family was outside, waiting on me to finish so we could hop in the van and drive three-and-a-half hours to a city where I was guest preaching the next day.

I was beyond "getting frustrated" to the point where I was literally thinking, *I'm not man enough to do this project. Men are supposed to be handy. My brother-in-law could do this. Why can't I do it? What's wrong with me? What will my wife think? What will my kids think? I'm going to have to buy a whole new kitchen table just because I'm not man enough to fix this one!*

Then, right on the heels of failing this project, I got in a van with five other people for a four-hour car ride.

But because of traffic, what should have been an easy road trip turned into a seven-hour family experience. With every mile of traffic, my temper got shorter. I typically preach on Saturdays and miss college football. But this was one Saturday when I wasn't preaching; I had planned the perfect day of the table project and watching college football in our hotel.

Eventually, I was so short with everyone in my van that my endlessly patient wife snapped at me. When her patience finally ran out, I wasn't exactly in my happy place, so I slammed on the brakes, pulled over, and yelled, "*You're driving!*" I slammed the door so hard that the interior of the door actually came off of the door and had to be snapped back into place.

As we sat in standstill traffic, my wife got out her phone and began furiously tapping it with as much anger as I've ever seen. I asked what she was doing and she said, "Buying you a train ticket! I don't want to be around you. I'm dropping you off in Norfolk and driving home! You can ride the train home after you're done preaching the gospel!"*

Well, she couldn't find a train ticket for me, so we drove in silence. We finally arrived at our hotel. We took our kids to the hotel pool and ordered pizza. There was so much tension, my wife and I were literally sitting on opposite sides of the pool as we ate our pepperoni pizza and smiled at our swimming kids. I did get to see the fourth quarter by the way. (My team lost. Go figure.) **

That day, my insecurity and anger got the best of me, and I kept making mistakes and hurting people. Just like the DIY project at home, I was trying to fix everything with my own solutions and wisdom, and it led to a hot mess. The reality is that we all do this in our walk with God and in the church. We convince ourselves that we know what's best, and we try to DIY grace and truth and community. But things almost never go as planned, and when that happens, our gut reaction is usually to bail or blow up.

————————————

*I don't think she actually said, "After you're done preaching the gospel." But that's what she was feeling. So I believe this is an accurate telling of the story.
**I shared this in a sermon once and someone said, "Carl, I love listening to you preach because you make me feel better about myself." Glad I could help.

Several years ago, a reality TV show did something that struck me as crazy. It involved a makeover where they gave the contestant cosmetic surgery and a new wardrobe. The ad guaranteed that it would change the contestant's life and destiny.

One woman was supposed to go on the show, but the night before her surgeries were supposed to begin, she was pulled from the show and sent back home. She then sued the show, saying she didn't want to go home ugly. The lawsuit said that in the prep for the show, producers had interviewed her close friends and family and coached them to focus on nothing except her physical flaws, even pushing them to verbally express their opinions on taped interviews that the woman later saw. There were no secrets, no hidden feelings, and no rewards.

What I found interesting was the reason they pulled her off the show. They had done all the prep and had put a lot of time into her, but the producers realized that her recovery was going to take too long. So, they sent her home. Essentially, they said, "You're *too* broken. We can't fix you on our timeline. So, you're out."[35]

> Have you ever been to that church?
> Have you ever been around that Christian?
> Have you ever *been* that Christian?
> I have.

And do you know why? Because it's easier to be around people who aren't bleeding. Think about it: When was the last time you were around someone who was bleeding? When was the last time you sought it out? It doesn't give me sleepless nights to pray for people whose biggest challenge is a promotion they're going after. It doesn't drain me emotionally to have conversations about someone's favorite Bible passage.

I've wondered before, "Why do Christians do that? Why do churches do that? Why do we say you have to get your act together *now* or you're out of here?" Then I realized that's what we do to ourselves. We tell ourselves things like:

- I'll try to get in shape but if I'm not a size eight by next month, I'll give up on the whole thing.
- I'll try to follow Jesus but if I get drunk one time, I'm obviously not cut out for that.
- I'll try to take control of my money but if I go over budget one month, I might as well not even try again.
- I'll try to fix a kitchen table but if it goes askew, I might as well never do another project at home again.

We tell ourselves: get it together now or don't even try. We feel this pressure to fix ourselves too. We watch one YouTube video, read one self-help book, or listen to one sermon, and think that's all we need to get our act together. But that is an anti-grace, anti-gospel mentality.

Jesus said to come to him if you're tired, worn out, or burdened. If I could get my act together on my own, I wouldn't need Jesus in the first place. So, this idea that once I come to him everything is sunshine and rainbows is just not reality. It wasn't reality for those who followed Jesus in the first century, and it's not reality today. We are not meant to carry the burden of fixing ourselves or others. No matter how long we follow Jesus, we will always need his grace, his truth, his freedom.

So, if I try to DIY my brokenness instead of bringing it up in community, it makes my brokenness worse, because I continue to fail, but I fail alone. Then I blame Jesus and his church, which makes me bitter toward both. We must create a community where we can embrace the awkward—the conversations, the confessions, the truth we don't want to hear—all of it. Only then will the renovation project on our soul be done right.

MENDED BY GRACE

On a recent Sunday at our church I had three great conversations:

- There's one guy who I check in with on a couple things, and one of them is his sobriety journey. So every couple weeks or so I'll ask, "How many days are we at?" and he'll tell me what he's up to. Last Sunday I go up to him and say, "How many days are we up to?" He appears anxious. Looks down. Shuffles his feet. After a long pause he says, "Well, I had a little setback. I've been sober one day." I said, "Okay, the worst thing Satan does to me isn't tripping me. It's convincing me it's not worth getting back up. I want you to get back up. I want you to get two. Let's get two." He smiled and said, "Alright."

- After service I was in the lobby and a guy came up to me who, last time I talked to him, said he was ninety days sober. I said, "That's awesome, keep it up." He came up to me and said, "Two things . . . pray for my surgery this week. But also pray because I messed up and I'm only two and a half weeks sober now." I said, "Deal."

- Right after that a few college students came up to me. I knew one of the girls; she introduced me to her friend. The friend said, "We gotta tell you, last night we got drunk and we had the best discussion about last week's sermon! We just love talking about theology when we get drunk!" Her embarrassed friend said, "Well, it was just a little tipsy, but it was a lot of fun." I clarified something for them but was glad they're on a journey with Jesus.

As I thought about those three conversations, I thought, *I love our church*. Because there are a lot of churches where you couldn't say that or you'd be looked down on, and you definitely wouldn't tell the pastor. But the reason I loved these conversations is that the biggest accusation religious leaders lobbed at Jesus is "Why do *you* hang out with *them*? Why do you hang out with people like *that*?" (author's paraphrase, Mark 2:16; Luke 5:30; 15:2). But I love Jesus' answer: "Healthy people don't need a doctor—sick people do" (Mark 2:17). I don't want to be part of a church where everyone walks around pretending to be healthy and no one gets help because they are afraid that they'll be looked down on or worse.

You can say a lot of things about the church, both good and bad. But when the church gets it right, one of the things you'd have to say is, we're the people Jesus hung out with. Because Jesus came to rescue lost and broken people—and that's who we are. Think about those people—two guys trying to get sober, two girls drinking and talking theology. They're in God's church. They're seeking. They're learning. They're growing. They're saying, "God, we're going to show up, and we're not going to stop showing up where you speak until you do something in our lives." And I think we need to follow their examples—not of their sin, but of their showing up.*

I can make you two promises about the church. One is that the church will let you down. The church is led by people, attracts people, is full of people. People are sinners. So, there is no doubt in my mind at some point the church will let you down. Someone will condemn you, someone will gossip about you, or someone will not help in a time of need. But the other promise I can make to you is that the church is what you need. Where else will you go to find a community of broken people? Where else will you go when you have been wounded? Where else will you go to find grace?

Winston Churchill once said, "It has been said that democracy is the worst form of Government except for all those other forms that have been tried."[36] I would say, "Church is the worst form of community,

---

*I'd like to think my sermons are good for discussion when you're sober as well.

except for every other form that has been tried." I know you may have been burned. I know you have questions. I know Christians and the church seem unsafe. But the things that make you sad and angry make Jesus sad and angry. We aren't meant to hide our brokenness or try to fix ourselves and others. We are meant to be like the people Jesus hung out with—openly broken and seeking grace. That is how true community is built.

Practicing vulnerability in church means being honest about your cracks and letting God and the community around you see the gold of God's grace over every area of your life. When I think about practicing vulnerability in the church, I'm reminded of a phrase used in the book of Hebrews: "See to it that no one misses the grace of God" (12:15 NIV84).

Do you know why the church exists? So that no one misses grace.

Why do we need the Scriptures? So that no one misses grace.

Why are we patient with sinners, including ourselves? Why do we sing worship songs? Why do we serve the community? Why do we listen before speaking? Why do we help up the person who falls in the same way so much so that it just drives us insane? So that no one misses grace.

Jesus came for broken people like us. Let's make the church a place of blood-stained pews. Let's learn how to embrace the awkward.

CHAPTER 6

BEATING UP BURGLARS

WE'RE ONLY AS SICK AS OUR SECRETS.

—ALCOHOLICS ANONYMOUS

Are you familiar with the PostSecret movement? In 2004, a guy named Frank Warren printed three thousand postcards with the challenge for people to anonymously mail in a secret they'd never shared before. He left them in libraries, subway stations, and art galleries. He started receiving responses and put them on a blog. This turned into a movement that is still going, and Frank has published over half a dozen books, highlighting many of the postcards he's received.

Many of them are funny:

"When I'm mad at my husband … I put boogers in his soup."

"Every time I get my toenails done, I want to kick the girl doing them in the face."

"I think women who don't wear makeup … are lazy."

"I love to pee when I'm swimming."

"I hate people who 'reply to all' on emails."

"I take extreme measures to poop in solitude."

"I give decaf to customers who are RUDE to me!"

But many are heart-wrenching:

"I wish my parents could see me for what I am instead of what I didn't become."

"I wish my father had forgiven me while he was still alive."

"I tell people I'm an atheist but I believe I'm going to hell."

"Sometimes I wish that I was blind, just so I wouldn't have to look at myself every day in the mirror."

"In my first marriage, I had better and more sex outside of marriage than in it. Some days, I feel like a heel and am guilt ridden. Other days I am grateful for everyone. They helped me keep my sanity. (P.S. I was a pastor.)"

"I haven't spoken to my dad in 10 years ... and it kills
my every day."

"Finding God is proving difficult."

"All of my life people have told me I'm not special ... I'm
very easy to replace. After 43 years it has finally sunk in.
I finally get it."

"My dad used to beat me and call it spanking."

"When I eat, I feel like a failure."[37]

What's your secret? We all have them. Maybe it's a desire that sounds
perverted to say out loud. Or an unspeakable trauma that brings you
shame. Maybe it's something that brings you joy that people think
is weird. Or an action from your past that still haunts you. What's
your secret?

When we talk of blood-stained pews, being open in church, and
sharing about our brokenness in Christian community, a lot of us have
a visceral reaction because we go to that thing. That thing is your secret.
It's the thing you don't want others to know. It's what you think of when
you hear the word "confession." It's what you think of when you hear
someone talk of being open. It's the thing you don't want anyone to know
and wish you could forget. If they knew you, they'd reject you. At least
that's what your fear says.

And when I say "that thing" I don't even necessarily mean it's something bad. Sure, it could be your worst choice or the thing that happened
to you that took your innocence, but it could also be a dream you have
or a relationship you want to heal. Either way, it's your secret. And by

keeping *it* closed off, it keeps *you* closed off. And you don't bleed, so you don't get well.

We keep secrets for all sorts of reasons. **What we want people to see is not who we are**, so we cover up. Our neighbor's marriage looks fine, so we don't tell anyone we're struggling. Our friends don't have a relative in prison, so we don't talk about ours. Everyone else acts like dating is so easy, so we downplay our fears or frustrations. John 3:19 says, "People loved the darkness more than the light, for their actions were evil." We don't want people to see something bad that would mess up our image, so we keep it in the dark. We'd rather portray a false image and have friends than expose our true selves and be alone.

We also keep secrets because **we're embarrassed**. Secrets often involve parts of us that have been hurt or are important to us. We can feel shame when we share our secrets with others. That's why these anonymous confessions are appealing—people have the benefit of sharing a secret without the embarrassment of others knowing who's confessing.

We keep secrets because **other people we've let in have hurt us**. If I shared something sensitive with one person and he told other people, you had better believe I'm not going to share it with someone else.

And sometimes we keep secrets because, frankly, **it's fun**! When you do things in secret there's an adrenaline rush to it. Proverbs 9:17 says, "Stolen water is refreshing; food eaten in secret tastes the best!" You may get caught. You have to sneak around. That rush can feel good. That's one reason people are attracted to affairs; because you're not supposed to do it, there's a sense of excitement.

On top of all that, Christians have a unique struggle with secrets. We're told we are supposed to be like Jesus—we're supposed to be holy. But even the most dedicated follower of Jesus still sins. We know how much people hate hypocrisy, so we think if our stuff becomes public the Christians will think, *Oh, he's not really dedicated,* and the non-Christians will think, *I knew it. Just what I thought: another fraud.* So, we convince ourselves we're being noble by not sharing our secrets.

WRONG THINKING

There's a phrase that creeps into our language that shows how we often get this wrong. The phrase sounds like a good challenge or even an encouragement, but it will take you captive and have you believing lies. It goes like this: "Act like a Christian."

This phrase is used both by followers of Jesus and those who reject them. We use it when condemning someone's behavior and describing how a follower of Jesus *should* have acted. People will say about a cheating husband, "He should act like a Christian." A teenager gets a DUI after drinking under-age and another parent comments, "He should act like a Christian." A single mom posts pictures of her at a wild party and someone comments, "I wish you'd act like a Christian." The problem is, when people say that phrase in that kind of context, it shows they have no idea what being a Christian even means, and they are trying to make the church into the exact opposite of what Jesus designed it to be.

What does it really mean to act like a Christian? Scripturally it does not mean that you act perfectly, because Scripture makes it clear that you are incapable of acting perfectly! If you could live perfectly, you wouldn't need Jesus, and there wouldn't be such a thing as a Christian. To be a Christian means you have recognized "I'm not good enough, wise enough, disciplined enough, smart enough to do life by myself. There's a dark part of me, and even if I hide it well, it makes me do bad things and think horrible thoughts, so I need Jesus to save me. I need to bring my darkness to the light." So, the phrase "act like a Christian" really just means to recognize you need help from Jesus. It has nothing to do with your ability to keep rules or act a certain way.

And of course, grace is not a license to sin. But you never get to the point where you don't need grace. When you first come to Jesus, it's all about grace; you growing with him is all about grace; and when you stand before him on judgment day, it's all about grace. So, to "act like a Christian" does not mean you are honest or disciplined or a hard worker—because I can do or be those things with or without Jesus. To act like a Christian simply means I have the humility to recognize I'm a sinner and desperately need the grace of Jesus to make me new, today and every day.

The progression goes like this: If we mistakenly believe to "act like a Christian" means we're perfect, then we keep secrets. Then we are a hypocrite. So, the very fear of hypocrisy turns us into the hypocrite we don't want to be.

Jesus once gave a stark warning about hypocrisy. Luke tells us that Jesus, in front of a large crowd, warns his disciples, "Beware of the yeast of the Pharisees—their hypocrisy. The time is coming when everything that is covered up will be revealed, and all that is secret will be made known to all. Whatever you have said in the dark will be heard in the light, and what you have whispered behind closed doors will be shouted from the housetops for all to hear!" (Luke 12:1–3).

Don't miss what he's saying: "All that is secret will be made known. All that's been whispered will be shouted." That's not exactly a comforting promise. But his point is, don't be hypocrites! See, we get it backward. We think, *I better not share because I'm supposed to be like Jesus, but I'm not. So, if I confess that thing, people will know I'm not like Jesus, and I'll make him, myself, and Christians look bad.*

However, Jesus says, "It's all coming out one day anyway, so get it out now!" The irony is that when we confess our secrets, we actually make Jesus look good, not bad. People see why we need grace. People see that we still need grace and that we're figuring out what grace and truth look like for the dark parts of us. People see that Jesus gives grace even for "that thing." So, in the end, what we wanted to hide actually drives people to Jesus.

What we're talking about is the ancient Christian practice of confession. Confession ensures we're more focused on showing others we need Jesus than on making sure we look good. The byproduct, of course, is that we create an environment where *other* people feel free to confess their secrets as well.

BEYOND HONESTY

As we talk about confession, it's important to understand the difference between honesty and openness. When we talk about secrets, we're not talking about simply being honest; we're talking about moving beyond honesty to openness.

For example, a pet peeve of mine is when someone asks, "Can I be honest with you?" What I want to say is, "Um, yes. I hope you're always honest with me. If you're not honest with me, we have no basis for a relationship whatsoever. So if you've been lying to me before now, what have we been doing here?!"

But when people ask, "Can I be honest with you?" what they really mean is, "Can I be *open* with you?" As in, "I haven't been lying, but I haven't yet been vulnerable." And being open is a requirement for a community of blood-stained pews.*

Recently my wife was hanging out with some of her closest girl-friends. There were about seven ladies there, all of whom know each other. And they're all honest, always. But as they sat around talking, catching up on life, one of my wife's friends said, "I need to talk to you all about what I'm learning with my counselor." Keep in mind this woman

---

*In case you're wondering, other pet peeves of mine include people talking while they have food in their mouths, glitter—in any context whatsoever—and when the Wendy's drive-thru lady only gives me two packs of ketchup for a large fry.

is fun, a strong believer in Jesus, a loyal friend with a servant heart. People love her.

But then her eyes got wet. She said, "You all know the pain I've had in my life—physical problems that stopped me doing the sport I like, I lost a brother to suicide, and I watched my husband almost die." At this point, tears are falling down her cheeks. "I'm realizing with my counselor that because of all the pain I've been through, I don't really open myself up in relationships because that would risk getting hurt. I've experienced so much hurt I just don't think I can handle any more. But I want to be open with you all because you matter to me." The tears continued to fall.

That's being open. She had never lied to her friends. But she went beyond honesty to openness. Being open, not just honest, is a huge key in building a community of blood-stained pews, because this is how people know you're really hurting.

Last year our church studied the book of Song of Solomon. I was excited to teach this book of the Bible, because it's all about a couple dating, getting married, and (in great detail) having sex. I knew it would really help people think about sex in a healthy way and prepare the singles with the right mindset.

As I prepared the series, I kept in mind that the biggest cultural trap connected to sex is pornography. It's accessible every moment of every day in everyone's pocket. The stats don't lie—pretty much everyone has been sucked in by this beast. I knew I had to share my story.

Being honest would say, "I had a long struggle with pornography." And that's fine. It's honest. It's a step. But it's sanitized. It's clean. It's easy. I knew I needed to be open, so I detailed the first time I saw porn: a cartoon in a Playboy magazine in sixth grade in the woods behind my friend's house. I can still remember how the sun was out that day, and how the vines swayed in the wind.

I shared that a gateway for me, and this is so embarrassing to write, was the Victoria's Secret catalogs that came in our mail. I'd steal them and look at them. Then we got high-speed internet, and my parents wisely put parental controls on. But I knew enough of their personal info that I could wait until everyone was in bed, then change the parental controls, look at what I wanted to see, then change them back.

Then I detailed the most embarrassing part, my breaking point. I was on a work trip on the West Coast with some other pastors. I had moved past looking at pornography, technically speaking, but with any sin we all have a line where we say, "As long as I don't ___, then I'm okay." And we all set our own line. With impurity, my line was, "As long as I don't look at naked people, then I'm okay." I fell into a habit during stress or loneliness of looking at pictures online of women in lingerie. At this gathering of pastors, that's what I did. Then I walked down to the lobby so I could attend a pastors' dinner.

There I ran into a friend of mine named Josh. And before I gave myself a chance to think twice, I confessed what just happened, and that it was a habit. Josh immediately said, "Carl, I forgive you." That felt good. But then he followed it with, "When you get home, I'm giving you twenty-four hours to confess this to your wife, and then I'm telling her."

I remember exactly where Lindsay and I were standing in the playground with the red equipment when I told her. I remember the swing my daughter was on when my wife started crying. I remember her look of shame when she couldn't make eye contact, because she thought she wasn't good enough to please me. It was a dagger.

Fortunately, my wife was gracious—truthful, but gracious. We did put helpful guardrails in place. I went multiple years without internet on my phone so I could learn to honor her with my eyes. But here's the point: I hated telling my church that. I hated telling you that. It's embarrassing. It's shameful. It's pathetic. It makes me feel like I'm not a real man or a good husband.

But bigger than my feeling of shame is my desire to know and be known. Bigger than my fear of being rejected is my longing to be part of a community that accepts me. Bigger than my feelings of not being a man is my desire to live in a community that will give me grace and show me the path to becoming the man God created me to be. And none of that can happen if I'm just "honest." It can only happen when I go beyond honesty, when I'm truly open about what's going on.

One of my friends has the strangest yet most striking way to start any small group he leads. On the first night of leading a group, surrounded in his home by people he's just met, my friend gets out his plastic dog poop. I'm not kidding. He bought it on the internet once upon a time. Then he gives a rehearsed speech. He says, "This group is a BS-free zone. We're here to be real. So, if you don't want to be real, you're in the wrong group and the wrong church. If we think you're giving us the BS answer, that you're not being real, we will throw this fake dog poo at you and call you out." Then he sets it on the coffee table in the middle of the wide-eyed group and says, "Let's open the Bible and get started!"*

I love that. One thing that must be true of the church is that we're real. It may be messy, it will sometimes be offensive, and it will often be difficult, but it will always be real.

———————————

Now that we know the importance of radical honesty in our communities, let's look at the things we need to confess to be fully known. Confession isn't just about telling others the ways we've sinned; it's inviting others in to see all the different sides of us so we can be as fully known and loved on this side of heaven as possible. Confession is meant to bring freedom, so if there's any area you need freedom in, that's a hint that you may need to confess.

*No, I have not asked him why he bought the fake dog poo, nor do I intend to.

THE SMALL STUFF

We're often attracted to the stories in church that are really dramatic and leave us thinking, *How did God rescue that person who was so far gone? That's amazing!* The consequence is that if something is making us bleed, we think it needs to be really dramatic before we're open about it. Otherwise, it'll sound like we're holier-than-thou, or maybe even that we're just pathetic since something so small would bother us. The reality is that confessing the small, even silly stuff can bond us in deep ways.

I have a friend who was trying to lose weight. He had done a good job, losing fifteen pounds so far in his journey. He was telling a close friend about it. The friend asked, "How much have you lost in total?" And my friend said, "Sixteen pounds." He lied. By one pound.

Later he was convicted of this, called his friend, and apologized. His friend said something like, "No big deal, that's still great!" But what I respected about my friend's response is that he freely told this story to other believers. And the reason I respect it is that the story is ridiculous. Lying over one pound? Look, there are about ten billion worse things in the world. So, when he shared it, he had to overcome that feeling of, "You will probably all think this is weird, but I'm going to share it anyway even though I feel stupid doing so." Is that what you feel? You have something you really want to get off your chest, or confess, or just say out loud, but it sounds so … dumb. But do you know what happens when you share your dumb, silly stuff? It builds true community. It builds trust, and people feel like they can let their guard down a little bit because the truth is, we all have small, dumb stuff that sticks around in our heads for far too long, and when the first person voices their small, dumb stuff, it sets a precedent.

Several months ago, my wife and I were getting ready to leave the next morning on a trip. We were flying to an event and packing our bags after the kids had gone to bed. As I was packing, I heard crying coming from one of my sons' rooms. This is not a regular occurrence, so at first, I thought I must not be hearing it at all. I went up to the door and listened, and, sure enough, he was crying. So, I went in and asked him what was wrong. He said, "Nothing." (Obviously not true.)

> I got in bed with him and asked, "My man, what's the matter?"
> Nothing.
> "Are you scared?"
> [Head nod.]
> "What are you scared of?"
> I don't know.
> "Are you scared about me and Mommy leaving tomorrow?"
> [Shoulders shrug.]

And what I was thinking in that moment was, *This is dumb! We travel a lot. We're going on an airplane; airplanes are safe. You shouldn't think that.* But then I remembered something, and I said, "You know what? I get scared too sometimes." He looked at me curiously. "Sometimes if Mommy is late and I don't know where she is, I get really worried that she's been in a car accident and got hurt."

At this point my son is looking at me like, "You are the weirdest dad ever. Why would you think that?" I talked about that for a few minutes, and what I really wanted him to know was "me too." I get scared too. You're not alone. I can't take your fear away. But I'm with you. And his fear went away because he realized he wasn't alone.

I guarantee you that when you share what may sound silly or dumb or immature to you, other people will not only respect that, but they'll also relate to it. And you will create a bond between you that is deeper than if you wear the mask.

THE RIDICULOUS DREAMS

Another thing we need to confess that may not be so obvious is the ridiculous dreams we have. Remember, we're talking about secrets. All secrets aren't sinful. But all secrets create barriers to true community. A community built on openness is about sharing everything. So yes, confessing sin, shame, and failure is necessary—but so is sharing the dreams and desires we have, even if they're ridiculous. This helps us build true community.

Here is my ridiculous dream: I have a fantasy about laying down my life for my family. And I don't mean in the daily, boring, what-Jesus-calls-us-to way that entails regular anonymous sacrifice. I mean in a spectacular way. The dream goes like this: Terrorists break into our house, hold our family at gunpoint, and say, "We're killing one of you." So, I look deep into my wife's eyes and with my best Liam Neeson voice say, "Then take me." My wife watches me give up my life in front of her. Then, for some unknown reason, the terrorists just leave our house, and my wife's last impression of me is of someone who died so that she could have life.*

I'm not sure what this says about my psychological makeup. There's probably some therapy needed in there somewhere. But here's what I've realized: other husbands think the same thing. I was scared the first time I verbalized this, but the immediate reaction was something like, "Oh yeah, I think the same thing—but in my fantasy I kill the terrorists with my bare hands before one of them stabs my heart with their dying breath. But my wife still sees me give up my life for her." Another guy said, "Mine is taking a bullet." Another said he wanted his wife to see him save their dog's life. Basically, every husband—I've learned—has this weird fantasy where his wife sees him as the hero.**

---

*Part two of this fantasy is that years later my sons grow up to become Navy SEALs. They hunt down the terrorists to exact revenge for their father, killing them one by one.

**Ladies, it's no use asking your husband what his fantasy is about impressing you. He'll lie and say he doesn't have one. (Unless he's reading this book with you.) But trust me, he's got it all planned out. It just sounds too ridiculous to say out loud.

Those are pretty ridiculous fantasies. But you know what? Everybody has them. And by "them" I don't mean every person has the same dreams. I mean every person has a ridiculous dream that when said aloud sounds dumb, childish, and ridiculous. But again, when you say it out loud, it creates a community where others realize, "Oh, I'm welcome here. All of me—even the ridiculous dreams I have are not off-limits here." And that's necessary if you want a community of blood-stained pews.

Much of the time, the secrets we are scared to share are not some deep, dark, shameful thing; they are just things we're embarrassed about. But when we share those things, we create a bond because other people feel those same things. They're afraid to share simple things too. When you share, it creates an environment where they feel safe to share as well.

It's amazing to me how this principle strengthens my marriage. I asked my wife once, "What makes you feel close to me?" She said, "When you tell me about your day." I knew that had to be a joke, so I sarcastically asked, "Like how I sat in the fast-food drive-thru and then dropped my keys and couldn't find them, and then had that bill to pay, so I looked stupid; and like how later at basketball practice that one kid got on my nerves; and like how after that I came home and told you all that at dinner?"

"Yep," she replied. And she gets it. She knows that sharing even small things draws people closer.*

THE DARK STUFF

Then there's the other end of the spectrum: the dark and heavy stuff. This is where we're so intimidated by how people may view us, how they will respond, what the consequences may be that we keep it in the

---

*Interestingly, the Gottman Institute has discovered that a baseline for a good marriage is simply knowing facts *about* your spouse, the small things, like their favorite color, favorite restaurant, favorite movie.

dark. We feel deep shame, so we keep it secret. But the only way we can experience the community we long for—the community where it's safe to bleed and others take care of us—is to bring our stuff, kicking and screaming, to the light.

When I decided to share my struggle with pornography, I was so nervous to share my dark secret with the church. I began by saying, "I'm maybe more nervous to share today than any sermon I've ever done. The reality is, what I'm about to share would get me fired from most churches." And I proceeded to share my personal struggle with pornography that stretched fifteen years. I hated it. I was embarrassed. I felt bad for my wife (who read it beforehand and endorsed it, but still). It was humiliating.

But it was also comforting, because sitting in our rows were hundreds of people who know what it's like to pursue porn, experience the thrill of an orgasm, and then despise themselves and be thrust into depression. For all those people it was a day of comfort and hope because they knew "This is a safe place for me. This is a place where I can bleed too." And even for the people who don't have that struggle, they have similar feelings about something else, so they too thought, *Maybe God's grace is big enough for me after all.*

I don't know what your dark thing is: past abuse, a shopping addiction, a mental health diagnosis; the list is endless. But I do know that until you are real with others, you will not and cannot experience full freedom and victory over that.

———

I love being a pastor, love my church, love my job. So, I have this habit that is, in a word, weird. A couple times a year I'll do an internet search of phrases like "pastor affair fired" or "pastor embezzlement" or something similar. Unfortunately, it always turns up fresh results. I'll read things like:

- A pastor who was known in his community for preaching against homosexuality with so much (angry) energy got arrested with a male prostitute.
- A pastor who got fired because it was discovered that he had a secret stash of church money that he could spend however he wanted—that amounted to millions of dollars.
- A pastor whose church went bankrupt and couldn't pay their rent, but the pastor drove a Bentley paid for with church funds.

And I could go on. The reason I search for that stuff is, frankly, to scare myself. I know those people are just like me. They're sinners who got into ministry because they love Jesus and are passionate about people finding grace and truth. But somewhere along the way they had a silly desire, and they didn't confess it. Then they fell in a small way but rationalized that it wasn't a habit. Then it grew into a really dark desire, but they thought, *If I bring this to light, other people will be disappointed in me.* So, they compromised, they sinned, they rationalized, and they fell. And it all started with hiding something. It always does. And that's true not just for pastors in the news; it's true for all of us.

The way you begin to share your secrets is with the small things and the ridiculous things. But eventually you must get to a point where you are sharing the hard things, the dark things. Have you noticed how much the New Testament speaks of light and dark? It's all over the place: Jesus came to light the darkness. People choose evil because our hearts are full of darkness (see Ephesians 4:18). You are children of the light, not darkness (see 1 Thessalonians 5:5). Take no part in deeds of darkness (see Ephesians 5:11).

Jesus brings light to the dark. He exposes our inner thoughts. And here's why: bad things grow in the dark. Darkness is where sin festers, the past cripples, and bitterness grows. Secrets thrive in the dark.

But confession leads to living freely and lightly.

I have sat with countless people before, mostly in the context of marriage, where one person is confessing something to the other. And the reality is, if they got the pastor involved, it's a big confession. But the weirdest thing takes place, every time. I don't even consider it weird anymore, because I expect it, and it makes sense when you think about it.

One person will have carried this dark secret for years. They have finally worked up the courage to tell the spouse. I'm involved because they're afraid for their life otherwise. And when the confession is uttered, I see the sinned-against spouse start to grieve. It may flesh itself out as anger, sadness, rage, or silence. But you can see a physical reaction taking place. And it's understandable.

What's interesting is, I also can see a physical reaction taking place in the confessor. They breathe easier. They're relaxed. They may be crying because of the pain they are causing or because they're nervous about the response they're going to receive. But every time you can plainly see relief. They've been carrying a burden they weren't meant to carry, and it's been heavy, tiresome, and crushing. It's made it difficult to go through a normal day because they're wondering when the nightmare of other people knowing their secret will come true. And when it's finally out, it's freeing.

Maybe this is why James said to confess our sins to each other so we will be healed (see James 5:16). Not only is confession freeing, but it also recalibrates us spiritually. Philip Yancey says it this way: "The approach of admitting our errors, besides being most true to a gospel of grace, is also most effective at expressing who we are. Propaganda turns people off; humbly admitting mistakes disarms. Far from claiming to have it all together, Christians regularly confess that we do not. After all, Jesus said he came for the sick and not the well, for sinners and not for saints. True followers of Jesus distinguish themselves primarily by admitting failure and the need for help."[38]

I believe sometimes we "sell" Jesus wrong. We act like Jesus will give you the perfect life if all you do is give your life to him, and that's *kind of* true. But you also have to practice confession. You have to bring stuff to the light. And this is not a onetime deal when you first come to Jesus. This is a lifestyle.

So, let me ask: What is a secret you've been carrying alone in the dark that you need to confess to someone else? What is the thing you are physically hiding? What is the memory you are suppressing? What is the fear you are not communicating?

You're not alone. We are all broken people. If you're part of a church, this is a chance for you to be part of a church with blood-stained pews. Think of it this way: if you sit in a pew with twenty-four seats across, here's what's true of the people in your row if it's full of average Americans:

- Two people struggle with clinical depression.[39]
- At least two, probably three people have used illegal drugs this year.[40]
- Three people are infertile.[41]
- Three women have been sexually molested.[42]
- Three men were sexually assaulted.[43]
- Two people are alcoholics.[44]
- Twelve—half—say that porn is a problem in their home.[45]
- Two have abused prescription drugs in the last year.[46]

And the more you recognize your own brokenness, the more likely you are to run to Jesus. So, the number of broken people in church might be higher than any other place we gather.

Remember what Jesus said: The time is coming when everything that is covered up will be revealed and all that is secret will be made known.

I know when you read that, some of you get a pit in your stomach. And you're hoping it's not true. But remember: Jesus died. He rose again. He's coming back. Your secrets will be brought to light. I'm not saying that to scare you; I'm trying to let you know there's a better way.

There is a time when I would've read Jesus' words and instantly my palms would start to sweat. My heart would race. I'd get fidgety. Because I had secrets, and if they came out, I'd be ashamed. But Scripture tells me: it's going to come out anyway. I decided I'd rather share it on my own terms.

Listen: being open is a better way to live! Hiding in the dark is ruining you. It's holding you captive, making you live in fear and carry a heavy burden. Your mind is full of questions: "What will others think? Will they reject me? What will my parents do? How will my spouse respond?" But it is much better to be free, to have nothing hiding in the dark. What's in the dark is controlling you, and only when you come to the light can you experience freedom in Christ.

THE POWER OF "ME TOO"

Because the practice of confession is so powerful, we need to briefly think of how to respond to confession. We don't respond with advice or judgment, but with empathy. That's why I believe one of the most powerful phrases in Christian community—and absolutely essential to a church with blood-stained pews—is "me too." This phrase has received a lot of attention in the last few years, as it's been part of a movement encouraging women who've been abused and taken advantage of to come out of the shadows.

This two-word phrase is perfect for that movement, but it's not just a catchy slogan; it's a way of life for the Christian. "Me too" communicates empathy. It communicates understanding. It communicates, "I'm not here to fix you."

We are hesitant to say these two words because we misunderstand them. When we say, "Me too," we are not saying, "The very thing you went through, I have been through as well." We don't mean, "The pain you are experiencing, I've experienced too." We don't mean, "What happened to you happened to me." What we mean is, "What your thing is doing to you, my thing is doing to me. I have shame too. I have anger too. I have questions too." When said with that tone, "me too" becomes a comfort. It helps me know I'm not alone. Because when we're in pain, we don't want someone to tell us what to do; we just need to know we're not alone.

There's one more *PostSecret* I want you to hear. It's the very last one of the book: "I've told all my secrets, and now I feel free."[47] There's a sense of relief when you tell your secrets to anyone, even if it's an anonymous website. The way you really get free, though, is through Jesus. So, let's be people who live in the light, not the darkness.

What is your secret? What do you hold inside and not let anyone know? What is the thing that you would be terrified if someone found out? The thing that would ruin your reputation, that you could be blackmailed over? Is it a mistake from your past? A past relationship? Is it a family secret? A fear? An addiction? Share it. As in, right now. Put down this book, pick up your phone, and call or text someone to share what you've been holding in.

Because we have grace, we can be upfront about how we fall short. Jesus doesn't want you to *only* experience eternal life in heaven when you die, though that would be enough. He wants you to experience freedom *now*. When you practice confession, you're on the path to freedom and healing. You're on the path to that "full life" Jesus talks about. Confess your secret. Then you too can say, "Now I feel free."

CHAPTER 7

FIND YOUR CREW

TO BE LOVED BUT NOT KNOWN IS COMFORTING BUT SUPERFICIAL. TO BE KNOWN AND NOT LOVED IS OUR GREATEST FEAR. BUT TO BE FULLY KNOWN AND TRULY LOVED IS, WELL, A LOT LIKE BEING LOVED BY GOD.

—TIM KELLER

I love a good reality TV show. Besides sports, the one show I've watched faithfully for years is *Shark Tank*. The premise is simple: an entrepreneur comes on the show to pitch their business or invention to the "sharks" to get seed money to grow their business, all for a percentage of ownership of the business.

I've seen some crazy things on *Shark Tank* over the years:

- The Licki Brush was a tongue-shaped brush you held in your mouth to brush your cat, so you were "licking them."
- Rounderbum was underwear, but not just any underwear. This underwear is padded, so your rear end has some extra volume.

- Potato Parcel is a gift you can send someone of a potato, with a picture on it—because that's something everyone wants, right?

But the craziest thing I ever saw on *Shark Tank* was an entrepreneur whose pitch went something like this: "Sharks, do you ever get home from a long day at work, you want to relax with a glass of wine with someone, but you have no one to share it with? And then you think: 'If only my cat (Yes, cat!) could drink wine with me, then I wouldn't be alone.' Well, sharks, now you can!" Then he proceeded to introduce his product—and I promise I am not making this up—Cat Wine.

The sharks laughed in his face until they inevitably asked the question that tends to be the death knell of bad ideas like this. They asked, "What are your sales?"

And that's when I about fell out of my chair, because the guy said, "We are on track this year to have 1.4 *million dollars* of sales!"

I thought, *Are you kidding me? People are so lonely that they are now drinking wine with their cats?!* Apparently, they are.* You've heard the stats—you know that through social media and the power of our phones we are more connected than ever, but we're also lonelier than ever. People are working more than ever. People in our country move to new states more frequently than ever before. Divorce and even not getting married to begin with are more common. People talk less in person and more online. And all of this leads to us being lonely.

Our society is becoming increasingly content with loneliness. But that is not how God built the church to function. Most of us are tempted to try to go it alone to protect ourselves and keep a semblance of control, but we need loneliness as much as cats need wine.

At this point in our journey, you may be thinking, *Okay, I need to*

*Note that there's no such thing as "Dog Wine." It's a cat-people thing.

deal with some stuff. I need to be vulnerable, but with whom? What do I share? Do I jump right into the deep end and share my deepest secret? Do I risk becoming the over-sharer that everyone avoids at parties? What if I sound stupid as soon as I start to share? I need a safe place to start all this, so where do I find that?

The thing is, to share safely, we need to put up guardrails and boundaries as we pursue vulnerability and openness in our communities. Boundaries and vulnerability are not diametrically opposed to each other. In fact, boundaries actually allow for healthier and safer vulnerability. We don't have many helpful examples of this, but the good news is that Jesus modeled vulnerability, accountability, and boundaries in his relationships with his disciples. If we want to be like Jesus in our approach to community, we must follow his lead into vulnerability.

One of the most practical things Jesus ever did in modeling great leadership and great relationships is found in Luke 6: "One day … Jesus went up on a mountain to pray, and he prayed to God all night. At daybreak he called together all of his disciples and chose twelve of them to be apostles" (Luke 6:12–13). I've skimmed right over this verse almost every time I've read Luke's Gospel, but one time, I was looking through the Gospels to answer the sole question "How did Jesus develop healthy relationships?" And a big part of that answer is found right here in these sentences.

Notice that it says Jesus calls together *all* his disciples. We don't know how many that is—fifty? A few dozen? A hundred? But we do know that it's more than twelve, because from that larger group of disciples (apprentices, followers), he chooses twelve who will become his apostles. Imagine the scene. It feels like a schoolyard pick for kickball teams: Jesus is the captain, and he needs to pick twelve guys out of, let's say, forty. He looks through the crowd and says, "I'll take you, and you, and I'll take you." Then when he has twelve, he says, "Okay. Everyone else leave, I need to spend time with just these guys." Seriously. He picked twelve and sent the rest home.

There's a huge lesson we need to get from this: Jesus was very intentional about his relationships. In fact, as you continue to study Jesus' relationships in the Gospels, you learn that there were essentially three groups of friends he had:

- Jesus had the *crowd* that was sometimes in the thousands.
- He had his *community* of twelve, who traveled with him, learned from him, and got to see a different side of him.
- But within the twelve was a more select *crew* of three. The three were the people he was closest to, the ones he let in to see him at his most vulnerable and at his most joyful. The three were Peter, James, and John.

Not long after choosing the twelve, Jesus is at the home of a young girl who has died. He takes in only Peter, James, and John. He heals the girl in a dramatic miracle, but nine of the twelve don't get to see it (see Luke 8:50–55). Sometime later, he goes up on a mountain and has a unique experience with God the Father that we call the transfiguration. But again, it's only Peter, James, and John who are with him—nine of the twelve don't get to see it (see Luke 9:28–30).

I want to make sure you're catching what Jesus did because this is so important for us if we want a church of blood-stained pews: Jesus had three circles of relationships. On the outside was the crowd. These are people who knew *about* Jesus. They liked him, they followed him around, many even worshiped him as the son of God. Inside of that, there was the community of twelve. This is who Jesus spent most of his time with. He taught them. He mentored them. He poured his life into their lives. But even within that, he had the crew of three: Peter, James, and John. These were the people that Jesus depended on in intimate ways. When Jesus was about to be arrested, to be tried and executed, he grabbed these three guys and said, "My soul is crushed ... keep watch with me" (Mark 14:34).

Jesus knew that to accomplish his mission of creating a church with blood-stained pews, he needed a crowd, a closer group of twelve, and an intimate crew. Jesus *loved* everyone—that doesn't mean everyone got access to him. Jesus came *to serve* everyone—that doesn't mean he could do it all one on one. Jesus came to change the world—he did that by pouring into a few.

The crowd got him in public. The community of twelve got the most time. The crew of three got the most intimate.

And we are no different from Jesus: we each need those same groups. But I want to focus on having a crew, because that is the group most necessary for deep vulnerability. We need that small group of people who know us intimately, who experience highs and lows with us, and with whom we can be 100 percent open. Let's break it down.

BUILDING YOUR CREW

You know those montages in superhero and action movies where the main character travels all over to assemble their crew? There's always cool music playing in the background and no words are exchanged—everyone just instinctively knows the deal. It looks good on the big screen for Tom Cruise, Mark Wahlberg, or a Marvel superhero. Unfortunately, that's nothing like real life.

Assembling a crew requires vulnerability. It's a process that takes time and, to remind you of our theme for this section, it can be awkward. The reality is, it takes work to build true community, but once you do, you can experience the joy and freedom of being fully known and loved. Then, when you have that community with blood-stained pews, you can truly live freely and lightly. So, how do we get to that point?

A first objection many of us have is, "I have no one to be open with."

I get it. This seems like a valid objection, doesn't it? I mean, if there's no one to be open with, you can't fault me for not being open, right? Although I use this excuse as often as I can, truthfully, it's just that: an excuse. I need to wake up to the reality of how vulnerability works.

Remember Jesus' circles of influence—the crowd, the twelve, and the three. You know how he got his twelve and his three? He initiated. He said, "Come and see." He let them experience who he truly was. In other words, he was vulnerable with them, and then they decided they'd follow him.

I do not like getting up in the morning, so I need some help. The problem, however, is Lew Wallace. Lew Wallace does not help my morning routine. Lew Wallace, if you don't know, was a general for the Union in the Civil War. He is the author of many books, including *Ben Hur*, which was later turned into the blockbuster movie. But in my book, Lew Wallace is best remembered for inventing a little button called the snooze button.

It used to be that when my alarm would go off in the morning, I would hit the snooze bar not once, not twice, but several times.* It got to the point where hitting the snooze button was such a habit that I would hit it without even waking up fully. Eventually, when my alarm did finally wake me up all the way, I'd look at my clock and be confused because I had no recollection of having hit the snooze. I had become so immune to my alarm clock that I could turn it off without even waking up.

Obviously, this was a problem because I would miss an appointment or a class. So, one day I got out a screwdriver, took apart my alarm clock, and broke the snooze button. I put it back together so that, if I hit snooze, it didn't stop the alarm. The alarm would wake me up on time, every time.

I believe the excuse "I have no one to be open with" is a spiritual,

---

*As a side note, am I the only person who thinks a nine-minute snooze is completely random?

relational way of hitting the snooze button. It's a cop-out: instead of facing what we really need to get done, we spiritually roll over in bed, cover our head in denial, and go back to sleep and not grow. So here are some tips to build a crew.

Start Slowly

To put ourselves out there, we need to follow a business principal taught by Jim Collins and Morten T. Hansen in their book *Great by Choice*. Imagine an old ship in a battle that has a certain amount of gunpowder. They don't start by putting all their gunpowder in one cannonball, because if they miss, they're done. First, they shoot bullets. Then when they figure out the exact trajectory and the right target, they'll fire a cannonball with all the gunpowder they have left, knowing they'll hit their target.

His point is that great organizations don't put all their resources into one thing, guess that it might work, and go for it. Instead, they test little by little until they have it figured out, then they put all their remaining resources into that thing.[48]

This is also how you get great community. You test a person with a little bit of information. You see how they respond. Do they gossip about you, or do they pray for you? Do they lift you up or make you feel worse? Do they quote Scripture to you or pontificate about their opinion? Then, over time, you figure out who is safe. Then you open up a bit more, see that they are still safe, and open a bit more, and on and on. After a few years have gone by, you realize you've developed a deep friendship.

Share Experiences Around God's Mission

One of the best things I did with my crew was go to an intense retreat in the Rocky Mountains. There were about thirty other participants I didn't know. But this was an *intense* retreat a mentor had recommended. *Everything* came out there. We spilled our guts in a safe environment to encounter God's grace and truth for our past so we could walk forward in the freedom of who he created us to be. But if I had gone with people who were in my "crowd," I could not have been vulnerable. I would've been on guard. I couldn't have bled. But it was safe to bleed in front of my crew, and it created a shared experience of God's work in us that will bond us for a long time.

Jesus demonstrates this with his crew in what we call the transfiguration. Frankly, it's a super weird story: Jesus goes on top of a mountain with his crew, and they see two dead people, Moses and Elijah. Then they hear God the Father say that Jesus is his son and to listen to him. Peter asks if they can stay there forever (and gets chastised for it), and before they head back down the mountain Jesus says, "Don't tell anyone about this." It was their little secret (see Luke 9:28–36).

But they got to experience the highs of being close to Jesus. They experienced his intimate relationship with the Father. They understood his mission a little more clearly than anyone else. They had a memory, a shared experience, that no one else ever would. That's how your crew is forged together too. Once you've shared with someone and begun building trust, sharing an experience around God's mission will bring you even closer.

Your Crew Sees Your Work in Progress

My mentor Jim Burgen is the best person I know at creating a culture of open brokenness, both in personal relationships and in a church at large. I asked him once, "How do you keep brokenness central to who you are as a church community, even as you grow?" His answer pierced me. He said, "Keep telling stories, and don't need a bow on it before you tell it."

Being openly broken means sharing your work in progress with your crew and sometimes with your community. Keep telling stories, and don't wait for them to have a bow on them before you tell them. I have never forgotten that, and I pray I never will, because it's easy to tell the story when it's all in the past. That's not vulnerability; that's just sharing facts. That's not a soldier getting help while he's bleeding; that's the soldier showing you the scar from when he bled twenty years before. This is the only way we can be held accountable for our struggles and actually experience spiritual growth.

The unfortunate reality is that many stories *won't* have a bow on them this side of heaven. Too often, we let the lack of a Disney fairy-tale ending lead us to limit the stories we tell or force us into a bad theology that ignores reality. I hope, I pray, that even though we continue to fall, if we are open about our brokenness, it leads people—mostly ourselves—to depend on Jesus more.

The bad thing about writing a book on vulnerability is, you have to keep sharing stories of how you've messed up; so here's another one. One of the primary ways I keep messing up is in controlling my temper with my kids. At the beginning of the school year, we were extremely busy as a family: church was entering a growth season; school was starting up; four kids were playing sports, which means four different practices each week and four different games every weekend; Saturday church and Sunday church; and work Monday through Thursday.

One Sunday, I decided that after watching the NFL game we would have some good family time, so we were going to the local state park for a family hike. We'd get out in nature, get away from the TV, and spend some time together. But on the way there, one of my kids had a bad attitude and then persisted in that attitude even after being corrected—and I blew up. It was an epic blow-up. I lost control—not physically lost control on my kid—but emotionally and verbally, I lost it. I literally thought, *I'm losing my mind here.* I screamed at my family, I turned the van around, we made the trip home in complete silence, everyone walked inside in shame, and our home was miserable the rest of the night.

I knew I needed to get right, so I got alone, decompressed, prayed, and got to a good place. A couple hours later, we all sat down to dinner. As we had our grilled chicken and broccoli, there was tension in the room because I was good, but I knew that wasn't enough. Each of us at that table was exhausted—exhausted physically from the first week of school and sports and church and parties and everything else, and exhausted emotionally because of the craziness between me and my kid. So I said, "Before we eat, I need to ask, Do you know what the word 'gospel' means?"

One of my kids said, "Does it mean Jesus died for us?"

I said, "Kind of. What it really means is I screw up but I'm not a screw-up. Jesus loves me. He forgives me. And he's going to give me endless second chances."

Then, I said, "I am ashamed of how I've been as a dad the last twenty-four hours. And I desperately need you all to forgive me."

It was so humiliating to say that, because I'm arrogant and insecure, and I'm supposed to be the man of the house. Everything in me wanted to run, to hide, to ignore and pretend everything was okay. But it was so freeing when they said, "We forgive you."

I don't know what my kids will remember when they're out of our house one day—if maybe they'll remember that one vacation or an epic Christmas. I know they'll remember dad losing it sometimes. But I hope and pray that they remember a home where we got in the arena, where we fought for our relationships, where we were real about our brokenness and how Jesus is redeeming us, where we didn't shy away from hard conversations because we were hurt or arrogant, but where we worked together to let Jesus work in us.

That's not fun. But that's real. And that's what I need.

Your Crew Calls You Out

A few years ago, one of our staff leaders came to me and said, "Carl, the message you want people to hear isn't getting across." I asked what he meant, and he explained what had happened at a recent church service. As volunteers were getting things ready, there was a major tech problem that would be a huge distraction. As hard as they worked, the volunteers couldn't seem to fix it. As the minutes ticked closer and closer to when service was to begin, my staff leader overheard a volunteer say, "Oh no, Carl's going to be pissed."

As my staff member told me this story, he said, "Carl, I think what you *want* people to say in that situation is, 'Oh no, we're not going to impact broken people.' Instead, they're living in fear of you."

I was crushed because I knew he was right. I knew the image I gave our volunteers was "I care about this more than you do, so don't mess up, and if you do, you're in my doghouse." And listen, it's not that I was walking around being a complete jerk. But when stress came, that's what got communicated.

I mentioned earlier the retreat I went to in the Rocky Mountains. To understand how this impacted me you have to know that one of the formational things in my growing up was my parents' marriage. I have this memory of sitting on the stairs, hearing my parents fight behind a closed door. I was paralyzed with fear and anger, and that was a defining thing for me.

I had a realization at this retreat that when I was a kid and my parents were going through marriage problems, the thought that went through my head was, *I wish I could control this. I don't like how this feels. If they would listen to me, they'd stop fighting.* What happened inside me is that I decided I need to control things. I couldn't articulate this as a kid—I couldn't articulate this even a few years ago—but the subconscious thought was, *If I'm in control, I won't get hurt.*

I realized that since I was ten years old, I've tried to control every relationship I've ever had in some way. To the outsider, it looks like I'm controlling because I'm arrogant and I think I'm right. But that's not it. The reality is, I'm controlling because I'm scared and I don't want to get hurt.

When I looked in the mirror, as we talked about earlier, here's what I realized: considering my growing-up years, I can say something most people I know *can't* say. I can say without a doubt that my mom loved me; I can say without a doubt that my dad was proud of me. (And those things are still true today.) I realized that if someone said, "We can give you different parents, and you won't have to deal with their problems and mental health issues and things will be easy," I'd say unequivocally, "No. No way. No thank you."

I know this is so elementary to most of you reading this, but I had to realize close relationships require the risk of getting hurt. In fact, I'll rephrase that: if you want a close relationship, you *will* get hurt, but it's worth it.

I had to go to that retreat with my crew to understand—and I hate when people say this, because it's so cliché—my parents did the best they could. Usually, I hate when people say that because I think they're lying to themselves. I know I haven't done the best I could—I'm working on it!—but my parents did do the best they could. I'm the one who said, "That's not good enough, so I need to control things."

I'm in the process (that I'm hoping isn't a *lifelong* process, but fearing it may be) of figuring out the difference between leading and controlling? I know I'm called to lead, but I'm learning I can't control.

I have figured out some ways I try to control others. I interrupt people constantly. I used to try to rationalize it like, "I know what they're going to say; I'll just save time." But if you dig down, I'm just trying to control the conversation. Another way I try to control is, I use the word "should" all the time, as in "You should do this": "You need a job? You should apply here. You need to get healthy? You should do this workout." I say "you should" constantly. Because I've trained myself to think, *If I can control things, it will be okay.* I'm working on those, but I haven't arrived yet. In fact, most days it seems I'm taking one step forward and two steps back. But I'm trusting Jesus to do his work in me.

As I type this section, my fight or flight mechanism is kicking in—my stomach is in knots. I'd rather tell you a story about going boating on the Chesapeake Bay or skiing in the Rocky Mountains. But I'm wounded and I need help. The only way for me to get that help is to acknowledge what's going on, and not just acknowledge it to God, but to acknowledge it to others.

Here's my point: I wouldn't have realized all this if my crew hadn't gotten on the plane with me to attend that retreat. It was only in the context of community that I felt safe enough to be vulnerable about my deepest wounds and, in the process, receive deep healing.

I'm so thankful for the community around me calling me out on the ways I wasn't honoring God. It's a hard and vulnerable thing to do, but it brings you closer together and invites God to grow you in an area you've been keeping from him. Because of being called out, I saw some brokenness in myself that I wasn't aware of, and in becoming aware of it, I was able to begin walking toward healing and allowing God's grace in that area of my life.

Your Crew Sits with You

One thing I love about Jesus is the fact that he always enters peoples' pain with them. When they are openly broken, he meets them with grace, and his presence brings healing. We need to do more of this in our communities—enter people's pain and just be with them.

When Jesus is about to be arrested, he's so overcome with emotion that Luke tells us his sweat was like drops of blood falling to the ground (see Luke 22:43).[49] But you know who was just a stone's throw away, who Jesus wanted near him in this overwhelming moment? Yep: Peter, James, and John.

I was talking with a friend who had watched his wife suffer from cancer and die at an age when she should've had decades of memories still to make. He said that in his pain so many people tried to be nice to him but unintentionally made things worse. People would send food over but it was food they couldn't eat. People would send gift cards but it was to places they didn't like. People would try to give advice, but that would just make them feel uncomfortable. He said what was most helpful was when he knew people were genuinely praying because that's when he knew he wasn't alone. He didn't need someone to "make it better," as if that were possible. He needed someone to lift up his pain.

Another friend of mine went through an ugly divorce. He felt like a failure, like he wasn't a true man, like he wasn't a good Christian. He sat on his couch for two weeks; he didn't want to do anything or go anywhere. But he had two friends who would bring him Chick-fil-A and just sit on the couch and watch TV with him. They didn't say anything. They didn't give advice. And for a time, that's exactly what he needed— just someone to enter his pain with him.

I've been trying to let my crew in more on these painful moments. It feels vulnerable to ask someone to sit with you in pain. But it's worth it. I remember doing this one night after receiving some criticism. It was the day after Easter, which is one of the biggest weekends of the year for me as a pastor. I work harder on my sermon; we have more guests and more services to accommodate more people.

That Easter, I had worked really hard on a sermon I thought would explain the gospel in a clear, relevant, and fun way. I preached at the seventeen-million services we had.* The services went great, and the next day I was enjoying a day off. And then I made a rookie mistake: I checked my email on a day off. Dumb, dumb, dumb.

I saw an email from someone I really respect and view as solid theologically, who's a friend on top of that. But when I opened the email, it was a scathing rebuke of what (he considered to be) an off-base sermon. Well, this immediately got in my head and made me think, *He's right. I have bad theology. I'm a bad leader. I'm a compromising preacher. The people I lead are in trouble. I should just give up now.* I spiraled into a dark place so quickly that I said to my wife, "I need to see my guys tonight." She agreed, and I texted them a brief synopsis and said, "Can we meet *tonight*?"

We all show up at the bar and as we are waiting in line to order our drinks, the first guy asks, "What did this email say?" I relayed the basics, and he immediately starts defending my sermon and me as a preacher. But I interrupted him to say, "I don't need you to defend my sermon. I need to be with people for whom the quality of my sermon doesn't matter." He got it. We moved on and had a great night together.

Your crew shares your pain. And whether you need advice or a distraction, they are there for you. They will bleed with you. They will carry you when you bleed. And when you experience that, *that* is what Jesus set up when he said, "I will build my church."

Your Crew Lifts You Up

I love baptisms. I love the public declaration of surrendering our lives and brokenness to God. But there was one baptism at our church that, in a way, was more memorable than the rest. This guy had started coming to our church when he moved, and we were the closest church to his new apartment. So, he could get to church in his motorized wheelchair

*Not an exact number. I lost count.

by himself, without having to depend on anyone. Every week he'd show up. I'd talk to him on occasion. Others got to know him as well.

Then when we moved to a new building, he figured out the local disabled mobility van would pick him up and bring him to church whenever he wanted, so he kept attending. Then he wanted to get baptized. After having a good conversation with him to ask what repentance looked like and what making Jesus his leader and forgiver forever would mean, we scheduled it.

But then we got stuck. See, we don't have some fancy baptistry that's easy to get in and out of. We definitely don't have a baptistry that has a special chair to help in people with disabilities. We have what is essentially a hot tub that has a high step over it. No way was he going to be able to get into that. Beyond that, he uses oxygen—a tube underneath his nose supplies extra oxygen to keep him healthy. One of our staff asked, "Steve, is this something you *can* do?"

And he was firm in his response: "I'm doing it."

So, we borrowed a big feeding trough that another church uses to baptize people. Because of his immobility, we recruited six grown men to lift this man out of his chair, set him down in the water, and then hear him confess Jesus as his Lord and Savior before dunking him, and having all six men lift him out again.

It was a labor of love. But you couldn't miss the metaphor—this is what Jesus does, and this is what church is. Church is the place that lifts you when you can't lift yourself. Church is the people who help you in your brokenness. Church is the community that comes around you when you acknowledge your need for help. And all Steve had to do was ask.

Think of the heroes of our opening story, Ken Moore and Robert Wright. For most of D-Day, one of them brought soldiers in while the other worked on the patients. Without two people working together there would have been no blood-stained pews. It's the same with us. Vulnerability does not exist in isolation. We must follow Jesus' example of having a crowd, a community, and a crew.

I love that old miniseries, *Band of Brothers*, that details the exploits of Easy Company in 1945 from when they began training to when World War II was over. The title of the series was taken from an old William Shakespeare quote, from *Henry V.*[50]

> From this day to the ending of the world,
> But we in it shall be remember'd.
> We few, we happy few, we band of brothers;
> For he to-day that sheds his blood with me
> Shall be my brother.[51]

That's what we long for—a community where we can bleed together. Paul often compared the Christian life to a race we run. Unfortunately, Jesus said many people won't finish the race. But if we are to finish, it will be because we did not run alone. It is not good for man to be alone.

You were created for community. Moore and Wright had each other. As you grow in a church of blood-stained pews, it is essential that you have a crew. Take a step to be vulnerable with someone today, because maybe, just maybe, that person will be your Peter, James, or John.*

---

*I had always wondered why Jesus chose Peter, John and James specifically. Someone pointed out to me that it seems Galatians 2:9 answers this. They were pillars of the church, probably (in my estimation) because Jesus made them his crew.

CHAPTER 8

I NEED TO KNOW HOW TO DANCE

THE TRUTH WILL SET YOU FREE, BUT FIRST IT WILL MAKE
YOU MISERABLE.

—JAMES A. GARFIELD

We are all familiar by now with the obesity epidemic in our country. We've seen the stats, heard the stories, read the articles. If you're like me, you go through phases of giving up certain foods, trying new sleeping habits, or experimenting with a new exercise routine—mostly based on the last documentary you happened to watch.

But recently I heard a new aspect to this. A newswire reported recently that doctors avoid discussing childhood obesity with parents. In the survey, 24 percent of doctors admitted feeling uncomfortable discussing a child's weight issues with the parents. This despite the fact that one third of all children are obese and obesity is now the leading cause of death in the United States.[52]

When I read that, I had two reactions to that story. One is sympathy.

I wouldn't want to be the doctor who has to tell a parent, "You have to do something because you're putting your child on a collision course with an early death." But of course my other reaction is—outrage is maybe too strong of a word, but . . . outrage! Because—hello!—these kids are on a collision course with death and you have a chance to stop it—you've got to speak up!

We've all been on the wrong end of someone using truth as a weapon, so we know it hurts. And we've probably all met Christians who think they are God's specially designated truth police, which leaves us with a bad taste in our mouths. So, it makes us not too keen on sharing hard truths.

When our church moved into the building that we now own and occupy, I got to share a few thoughts with everyone in the opening service. I explained how we had empty seats for the first time in a while and that reminds us of our mission. I pointed out the tub where we baptize people to remind them that our building will always be a place of grace. And then I mentioned that there is a little crawl space under the stage, primarily used for running cables. But I had opened it up prior to the building opening and put a Bible in there, directly underneath where I or anyone else would stand when preaching. And the idea, I explained, is that we always need to stand on truth.

I felt pretty good about myself after explaining that, thinking it was a cool metaphor. But then our guest speaker, Jim Burgen (who told me to tell stories before they had bows on them), got up there, and the first thing he said was, "Listen, I love that you stand on God's Word. That's good. That's important. But please don't take God's Word and use it as a weapon. Please don't take that Bible and hit someone over the head with it, because too many Christians have experienced that, and it turns them off to Jesus."

This book is about being open about our brokenness, about choosing to be vulnerable in Christian community so we can experience the life-giving benefits of a community that has blood-stained pews—one that is a safe place to bleed, a safe place for the wounded and broken. The problem is, too many of us have chosen openness at one time or another, and instead of receiving grace rooted in truth, we received condemnation that was rooted in judgment and disguised as truth.

We have to live in the truth. But please keep in mind, we're not talking about serving as the truth police for other people. Yes, the Scriptures teach us to speak the truth in love. But it almost takes a PhD in following Jesus to do that well. We're at 101 stuff here, which is choosing to live in the truth ourselves, choosing vulnerability within Christian community, and being the person in those blood-stained pews.

As we practice vulnerability, it is not enough to practice confession and live in community. Another way we must embrace the awkward is to choose to live in the truth. And to do this, we need to model Jesus' truth to people, so let's look at a few characteristics of Jesus' truth.

JESUS' TRUTH IS HELPFUL

I was at the gym several months ago after yet another mass shooting. I was watching CNN while on the treadmill, and right when I started watching they interviewed a local pastor, who looked young. His T-shirt was trendy. He was articulate. I thought, *This is a fantastic opportunity— this guy has a national TV audience where he can bring true hope to a horrible situation!* They asked him a few generic questions and he was talking about how the community is trying to draw together and lean on each other, and that was all fine and good.

But the longer he talked, the madder I got, because he wouldn't really say the problem and he didn't ever say the solution. At one point the reporter straight up asked him, "What is the problem here?" And he said something about how young people feel too alone, and they're too isolated. While I agree that people are alone and isolated, he neglected to talk about the root problem, which is sin! When the sin nature, that we all have, goes to the darkest of dark places, the full expression of that is horrible things that hurt people. Mass shootings happen because of sin.

So then when the reporter asked this pastor what needs to be done, he said, "We need to provide community for young people." And at this point I was getting fired up on the treadmill, because the only answer for sin is the blood of Jesus Christ. The only thing that can overcome death is Jesus. The only thing that can heal hate is grace.

Mark Batterson articulates the problem with this young pastor's answers well:

> The challenge is that we live in a culture where tolerance has been elevated above truth. It's considered wrong to say that something is wrong, and I think that's wrong. I certainly want to be known more for what I'm *for* than what I'm *against*. And truth shouldn't be used as a weapon. But to think that everybody is right and nobody is wrong is as silly as pretending that everybody wins and nobody loses. Come on, you know the tee-ballers are keeping track of the score! And even if *not* keeping score works for one season in Little League, it doesn't work in the real world. When truth is sacrificed on the altar of tolerance, it might seem as though everybody wins, but in reality everybody loses. God calls us to a higher standard than tolerance. It's called truth, and it's always coupled with grace. Grace means: I'll love you no matter what. Truth means: I'll be honest with you no matter what.[53]

I realized the reason I was getting so mad is because I was so sad! What needed to be said is, "In tragedy and pain, there is a God who loves you and who can redeem you. His name is Jesus and he died to set you free from sin and guilt and shame. You can walk in grace, hope, and purpose." As Jack Miller said, "You're a worse sinner than you ever dared imagine, and you're more loved than you ever dared hope."[54]

The point is this: in that terrible situation, people needed hope. But true hope, helpful hope, in the darkest of situations only comes when you speak Jesus' truth.

JESUS' TRUTH IS ETERNAL

One reason we want to ignore Jesus' truth and do whatever we want is, it sometimes seems Jesus' truth is outdated. Too often it seems like God's "truth" is really more like those dumb laws you've read about before. You know what I mean? Every so often you'll hear a list of laws that apparently (maybe?) made sense once upon a time, but now they're outdated at best and downright obtrusive at worst. Here are some of my favorites:

- In Baltimore, it's illegal to take a lion to the movies.[55]
- In Illinois, you can't give lighted cigars to your pets.[56]
- In Pennsylvania, "Any motorist driving along a country road at night must stop every mile and send up a rocket signal, wait ten minutes for the road to be cleared of livestock, and continue."[57]
- In Nicholas County, West Virginia, "no member of the clergy is allowed to tell jokes or humorous stories . . . during a church service."[58]

We hear of laws that mattered once upon a time but are clearly outdated and we think, *Maybe God's truth is outdated too.* We even see this with books of authority. The manual for professional mental health workers is the *Diagnostic and Statistical Manual of Mental Disorders*, or DSM for short. It's a thick book that has been compiled and edited over the years by mental health professionals. Basically, it lists and describes every possible psychiatric mental illness you can have. It's a very helpful tool to professional clinicians.

But here's the problem with it: it's always changing! One expert said of the most recent version, "Half the population will have a diagnosable disorder in their lifetime."[59] Some examples of the new ones are: if you often over-eat, that's now Binge Eating Disorder; children with temper tantrums suffer from Disruptive Mood Dysregulation Disorder; there is now a Hoarding Disorder; and finally Caffeine Withdrawal is now a disorder.[60]

I'm not a fan of a lot of this because I think it minimizes true mental illness. I don't like rationalizing away my kid's tantrum as a disorder because it de-legitimizes those with deep disorders. Don't miss my point. I go to counseling; if you need medicine from your psychiatrist, please get those and take them.

The DSM changes. And I need a standard that's not going to change in five years, unlike the DSM. We need something unchanging to guide us. Thankfully, "Jesus Christ is the same yesterday, today, and forever" (Hebrews 13:8). That's the kind of truth I need. The kind of truth that says, "I *am* the truth." It's not, "I *was* the truth," or, "I'm the truth *for now*." He says, "I *am* the truth." It's present—it's now and forever.

JESUS' TRUTH IS RELEVANT

I heard a story once of a dad helping his son with math homework. The son was struggling to study for a math test that he needed to do well on and the dad was encouraging him to study. But amid their frustrations about equations the son said, "Dad, I don't need to know this. I *really* need to know how to dance."

Apparently, the school dance was coming up, and while the teenager couldn't for the life of him figure out why cosine and tangent would matter in his future, he was scared to death of looking like a fool in front of the ladies on the dance floor.

The way some people talk about the Bible, you would think they're teaching algebra in a world where you just need to dance. There's an old saying that information without application is an abomination. I agree. I'm a big fan of studying theology, but I also know that theology has to be practical. Truth without a "so what" leaves us saying "who cares?"

The reality is, Jesus' truth is relevant. He talks about how to handle my enemies, my sexual desires, my money, my family members, and on and on. It's why he teaches in Matthew 6 to pray for our *daily* bread. Jesus meets our practical needs in the here and now.

In my experience, the area of life we most want to keep to ourselves for fear of what God's truth will be is anything related to sexuality. A lot of us try to convince ourselves that God's truth isn't relevant in this area anymore. In fact, when I teach on any aspect of God's plan for sexuality, I get complaints that the group I'm teaching shouldn't and can't follow God's truth. That applies to homosexuality, purity while single, being faithful in marriage, gender identity—any of it. So, I have to remember we're all in the same boat here. We *all* struggle to follow God's truth when it comes to sexuality. To know that, I just think of my friends.

- I have a friend who's never had an orgasm—and not for lack of trying.
- I have a friend who was raped by a family member and can't have sex without thinking about that.
- I have a friend who's looked at so much porn that when his wife comes on to him, he says, "I'm sorry. I can't get excited for you—you're not hot enough."

- I have a friend whose spouse had an affair and then they went multiple months without sex.
- I have a friend who has gay hookups and feels completely ashamed and worthless after because he's married.
- I have a friend who was molested. She's been married over five years and has never had sex.

You know what those people need? Yes, grace. Yes, endless second chances but they also need truth. They need to hear truths like:

- What that person did does not define you.
- Who you are is more important than what you do.
- What happened in the past is not a prison you have to stay in.
- Physical therapy can help you.
- You are God's child, and that defines who you are, not what happens or doesn't happen in the bedroom.

Jesus wants to set you free. Jesus will set you free. But you must be open about your wounds, or you won't experience the freedom he offers.

––––––––––––

Jesus said, "I am the truth … and the truth will set you free" (John 14:6; 8:32). As we seek Jesus' truth within the context of community, it will sometimes be painful, embarrassing, and maybe even depressing: in a word, it will be *awkward*. But when we are in a community founded on grace, Jesus promises it will also always be freeing.

The problem is that what a lot of us do is have off-limits areas. We say:

- "Jesus, I'll be vulnerable and open about everything, except for my career."

- "Jesus, you can give me some truth about lots of things, but not about sex."
- "Jesus, I want your advice on how to live, but not regarding money."

So, we live in this kind of pseudo-community where it feels like we're open and other people think we're open, but we have this one thing, this one area, that is off-limits to Jesus and other Christians.

Sometimes our off-limits areas can be big, dark secrets, but the off-limits areas are often what I call acceptable sins. I don't mean they are acceptable to God, but as Christians we sure act like they're acceptable. Here are a few of the more common acceptable sins:

- Worry. We disguise this by calling it "wise concern" or talk about things we're praying for, but often that's a cover for obsessing over something outside our control. But Jesus said, "Don't worry about anything."
- Workaholism. Jesus said the Sabbath was made for us, not vice versa, meaning he wants us to have a rhythm of rest. But when is the last time you confessed to another Christian that you had worked seven days in a row without an email break?
- Addiction to caffeine. Paul says, "I won't be mastered by anything," but how many of us brag about what we're like before our morning coffee?
- Gluttony. This is my personal favorite. For the record, gluttony is not the same thing as being overweight, although there's often overlap. Gluttony happens when we neglect to treat our body as a temple and go with the mantra "If it feels good, do it," or maybe better: "If it tastes good, eat it!"

Think about it: when is the last time you were with some Christians and one of them said, "I need to confess to you all that I've been eating as much as I can because it tastes good." When is the last time you heard a Christian say, "I cannot function without caffeine. I've created dependence on a drug"?

I know what you're thinking: *Come on, Carl, drinking coffee isn't that big of a deal*, and I think the same thing.* But my point isn't to rail on those things. My point is, we draw a circle around our favorite indulgence and say, "Jesus, that's off-limits." This is what you see in Jesus' interactions with people in the New Testament too—they have things that they hold onto, and Jesus tells them that sacrifice to him in every area will lead them to abundant life and true freedom (see Matthew 19:16–30; Mark 10:17–31; Luke 18:18–30).[61]

Think back to our story of D-Day with Privates Wright and Moore. Their job was to care for the wounded. We know they treated around eighty that first night in the Angoville church. We don't know how bad the wounds of those specific soldiers were. But we do know there were 15,000 soldiers in World War II who had "major amputations" because of injuries. In other words, 2.5 percent of battlefield injuries resulted in amputation.[62] So it's likely that Moore or Wright had to tell multiple soldiers, "Your limb will need to be amputated at some point." They had to dole out some bad news.

But doctors do amputations because there are cases of disease, poor blood flow, or other issues that make keeping the limb detrimental to the survival of the patient. So, the doctor says, "We've got to cut this part out if you're going to live." It's a harsh truth, but it leads to life.

And Jesus does the same thing for us. He gives us hard truth after hard truth. But he also promises, "Following me leads to life."

---

*If you were paying attention earlier, you realize you can cop out by saying you just have a diagnosis of Caffeine Withdrawal. It's now a disorder, you know.

We live in a culture where there is an epidemic of dishonesty, half-truths, and—if we call it what it is—lying. Satan is the father of lies, but Jesus calls us to a higher standard. If we want to create a culture where it is safe to bleed, we can and must embrace and live in the truth. I can promise you that it will be awkward, but I can also promise—because I have an empty tomb to back me up—that the truth will set you free.

CHAPTER 9

LEAP OF FAITH

DO NOT FOLLOW WHERE THE PATH MAY LEAD. GO INSTEAD WHERE
THERE IS NO PATH AND LEAVE A TRAIL.

—UNKNOWN

Many American companies are so afraid of getting sued that they go
to great lengths to protect themselves, and sometimes this results in
insanely stupid warnings on everyday products. In fact, there's something called the Wacky Warning Labels Contest that gives awards for the
most "absurd and silly [warning] labels" attached to everyday products.[63]
Here are some recent winners:

- The Grand Prize Winner was for a globe with the warning:
  "These globes should not be referred for navigation." I'm just
  picturing Gilligan holding up a decorative globe.
- The Second Prize Winner was for an electric razor for men
  with the following warning label: "Never use while sleeping."
  Wait, what?

Here are some past winners I read about:

- "Harmful if swallowed": a warning on a brass fishing lure with a three-pronged hook. (Knowing how much some fishermen drink, this one does kind of make sense.)
- A warning label on a small tractor said, "Danger: Avoid Death." (Umm, yes, we agree.)[64]
- A warning label for Nytol One-a-Night sleeping aids said, "May cause drowsiness." (That's the point, right?)
- A rotary tool (aka: a drill) included the following warning label: "This product is not intended for use as a dental drill." (Maybe the fishermen had this one too?)[65]

There are some stupid warning labels out there, but I do feel compelled to share a warning here. We've had all this great talk of vulnerability and how Christian community is a safe place to bleed. But here's the hard truth: it starts with you. Everyone wants to be part of a community that is open and vulnerable. The problem is, someone has to go first. And you know who "someone" is? You.

If you've seen *Band of Brothers*,* you remember that Dick Winters was the leader of Easy Company in World War II. When I read the book detailing his firsthand account of what happened in the war, I was struck by the contrast between the leaders he witnessed. One story in particular jumped out at me because it shows the contrast between someone who was willing to go first and someone who wasn't.

In the battle of Bastogne, they are mounting an offensive and will be able to win the battle. Lieutenant Dike is over Easy Company and is supposed to be leading the charge. But right at the perfect time to charge, Lieutenant Dike freezes. He won't move, and his company becomes sitting ducks.

Winters is watching this from behind and he wants to go lead the

---

*And if you haven't seen it, we can't be friends. Seriously, go watch it today.

charge himself, but he knows he can't neglect the other companies, so he calls Lieutenant Speirs and says, "Speirs, relieve Lieutenant Dike! You're in charge of Easy Company now."

Spears sprints—under fire—to Dike and says, "I'm in charge now."

They need to communicate to I company, so instead of sending someone else, Speirs himself sprints through no-man's land to I Company. Once he communicates with them, to everyone's shock, under gunfire, he sprints *back* through no-man's land to Easy Company. He tells them what to do. Then he leads the charge, and they win the battle.

That picture of Lieutenant Dike vs. Lieutenant Speirs was striking, because one of them was only concerned about playing it safe. The other was concerned about leading his men. In a way, that picture is what we're talking about: are you going to be Lieutenant Dike or Lieutenant Speirs? One fears getting hurt and does nothing. The other knows he could get shot at but does the right thing to lead anyway.[66]

What we're really talking about is being like Jesus. Jesus one time very simply states, "For even the Son of Man came not to be served but to serve others and to give his life as a ransom for many" (Mark 10:45). Often, when we talk about serving, we refer to the physical acts of serving: doing good deeds in your community, performing practical acts of service for your spouse, being a good Samaritan to the down and out. And those things are undoubtedly part of what Jesus is referring to.

But have you ever considered that the way Jesus served us was in making himself vulnerable? Think about it: he made himself physically vulnerable by experiencing the pain of execution via crucifixion. He made himself emotionally vulnerable by experiencing the disappointment of his best friend betraying him. He made himself relationally vulnerable by opening his heart to his disciples, only to see them confused or jealous. He made himself spiritually vulnerable by weeping about his destiny in front of his closest friends.

Even the statement we just read from Jesus is him being vulnerable. It comes on the heels of his disciples arguing about which of them is most important. Jesus has to correct them by saying, "Guys, remember what I do. Remember what I've taught and what you've seen from me." It's a very vulnerable moment (see Mark 10:35–45).

Here's the problem with being part of a church of blood-stained pews. We all want to be a part of it, but none of us wants to cause it. None of us wants to go first. We're fine with hearing the other person talk about how they are hurting, doubting, or recovering, but we want to keep our doubts and our anger to ourselves. And I get it—it could backfire! The word "vulnerable" essentially means "to wound." When I'm vulnerable, it means I'm giving you a loaded gun and trusting you won't use it to shoot me. But the reality is, I only find out if you'll shoot *after* I give you the ammo.

So, the question is, will you be Lieutenant Dike or Lieutenant Speirs? Will you risk being shot at to lead people to a new reality, or will you cower in fear, knowing that's the only sure way to protect yourself from being shot?

Ken Moore and Robert Wright had to go find people who'd been shot in order to save lives. And in order to find people who'd been shot, they had to risk being shot! They had to go out into the middle of the battle. If they had sat around in that empty church, waiting for the wounded to magically find them, they would have helped no one, healed no one, and made no impact. It was only by going out into the battle and risk being wounded themselves that they could help those who had been wounded.

Here's the reality: the people around you want to experience a community where they can be open about their brokenness. They just need someone to go first. That someone is you.

ALL IN

Do you ever watch those poker tournaments on TV? There's a group of people in a dark room, half of them wearing sunglasses, and we get a peek at their cards while their opponents decide to bet or fold. Inevitably there is the moment when one of them says, "All in," and you know someone is about to become a winner. There's nowhere else to hide, this is the final call, everything is on the line. To initiate well, you have to go all in. You can't "kind of" be vulnerable. You have to be truly vulnerable.

I recently read a book from a well-known Bible teacher on dating, sex, and marriage. I was hoping to get some tidbits I could use, so when I got to a chapter on conflict, I was excited to learn from this man I look up to from afar. But I didn't find anything. Here's why: The guy who was writing it—again, a famous Bible preacher—to set up the chapter on conflict said that he and his wife have conflict. At this point I lean in, thinking, *Me too!*

He went on to describe that sometimes on the interstate his GPS tells him to take this exit but he thinks the next exit will be faster so he ignores the GPS, and his wife rolls her eyes at him.

And that was it—that's his big conflict! When I read this, I literally took the book and threw it at the wall because I realized, "You're either lying to yourself, or you're lying to me, or I just can't relate to you."

Listen, if your biggest problem in life is your spouse every now and then rolls their eyes at you—I'm happy for you, really. The rest of us need Jesus to give us deep help. We have marriage problems, and this legal thing, and this bullying thing, and that physical thing, and the relationship that constantly hurts—we need the power that raised Jesus from the dead because our lives need that level of help.

My mom and dad have been open with me for years about their marriage and the struggles they had, mostly when I was very young. My mom told me once that years ago when these struggles were at the worst, there would often be weeks when she metaphorically crawled into church, hoping for just a little something to get her through one more week.

If, during their struggles, a pastor got up and said, "We're going to talk about marriage conflict today," she would've leaned in and started taking notes. But if the teacher's worst example of conflict was, "My wife rolled her eyes at me," my mom would've walked out because that teacher couldn't relate to her. She needed someone to bleed in front of her, someone who was hanging on to Jesus, to know she could do the same. And that principle is not just true for the preacher on a stage or the author of a book. It's true for you in your circles of influence.

The apostle Paul says, "You should imitate me, just as I imitate Christ" (1 Corinthians 11:1). At first glance, that sounds arrogant! It comes off as, "Hey you minions over there, I'm so much like Jesus that if you want to know what he's like, just follow me." But knowing what we do about Paul's character, I think the better way to interpret it is more like this: "Hey everybody, I know you're struggling to follow Jesus every day. If you need an example, just follow me. I'm not perfect, but I do walk in grace and truth. I'll lead the way." It's not arrogant; it's helpful.

When you initiate the sharing, it's not arrogant. It's not saying you have everything figured out. It's just saying, I want to live in a community where we help each other, so I'll show that I need help by going first.

JUST SHARE SOMETHING

Then the question is, what do I share? Do I dive right into the deep end? What if I don't have some big struggle in my life right now? Do I make something up? Do I exaggerate a doubt or fear or question? Where do I draw the line of what to share? Do I start with my biggest secret off the bat? Do I share my biggest sin from the past decade? Do I tell people how messed up I think my spouse is, or kids are, or boss is? What if that gets back to them? What if the problem is actually me, and I rant but then look selfish and stupid? What if I *am* selfish and stupid? When I have chosen to open up in the past, it sounds ridiculous as soon as it comes out of my mouth. Will that happen again? Maybe I should just keep my mouth shut because I don't know what to share.

Here's how we conquer this objection: just pick one thing. That's it. Pick one thing to share and see what happens. It's kind of like the jam study. Have you heard of this? I first read about the jam study in the book *Paradox of Choice* by Barry Schwartz. Here's a simple story that explains the principle:

> Researchers went to a gourmet food store and set up a display featuring a line of exotic, high-quality jams. Customers who came by could taste samples, and they were given a coupon for a dollar off if they bought a jar. In one condition of the study, six varieties of the jam were available for tasting. In another, 24 varieties were available. In either case, the entire set of 24 varieties was available for purchase. The large array of jams attracted more people to the table than the small array, though in both cases people tasted about the same number of jams on average. When it came to buying, however, a huge difference became evident. Thirty percent of the people exposed to the small array of jams actually bought a jar; only three percent of those exposed to the large array of jams did so.[67]

When they were overwhelmed with choice, they did nothing. They thought, *I might get the wrong one, so I'll just get nothing.* When people tasted six, they could figure out which one they liked and would buy one.

But when they had twenty-four to choose from, they thought, *Well, I may choose wrong,* so they wouldn't choose anything at all. It's the paradox of choice—if we have so many choices, often we do nothing.

When we are faced with a lot of choices, human nature is to do nothing. That impacts us with vulnerability, because there is a seemingly endless number of things we could share with people—things that would leave us "bleeding" in front of them. But here's the remedy to the paradox of choice: just pick something. That's it. Just pick one thing. It doesn't have to be your biggest, darkest secret (yet). It doesn't need to be everything you struggle with. In fact, if you share everything right off the bat, that's probably in the category of "emotional vomiting" rather than "vulnerability." Just pick one thing you are nervous to share, share it, and see how it goes.

LEAP OF FAITH

Have you ever heard of the "faith pole"? The camp I attended growing up had this. They considered it a fun activity; I considered it a torture device. It was essentially a telephone pole thirty feet in the air (that might as well have been 200 feet high). You strapped on a harness, shimmied up the pole, balanced on an approximately four-square-inch circle, and then you jumped out into the air, where a trapeze bar was suspended.

The harness you wore was connected to two ropes that were supported by pulleys and then held by your cabin counselors down below. This was terrifying to twelve-year-old me.* The problem was peer pressure! So, I strapped on the harness and climbed up. When I finally balanced on the top of this wobbly pole, there was no good option at that

---

*I don't have an irrational fear of heights; I have a *rational* fear of heights, meaning: if there is a steep cliff I could fall off and die or get injured, I am rationally afraid of going close to that. I don't freak out on airplanes because I know that would be an irrational fear. But I also don't go looking for poles in the air to jump off because that, well, doesn't seem rational.

point. You climb down like a wuss, or you jump into midair, hoping the counselors you ticked off the night before hold the ropes.

So I was standing there, staring into the open abyss before me, wondering, *Is this really worth it?* You know what I felt in that moment? Something I like to call the "bubble guts." It's when you get that feeling in your stomach of "I think I know what I need to do, but I really don't want to do it because I'm not sure it's worth it!"

But faith is taking a risk. It's taking the leap. It's jumping into the unknown. Now, it's not completely foolish risk; it's risk based on what's happened before, the information you know, and awareness of would could be. Faith is calculated. But faith always has action. One New Testament author says faith is being certain of what we do not see (see Hebrews 11:1). And being certain looks like taking action. For example, you can say you have faith that I'm a good driver, but if you won't get in the car with me, you don't really have faith in that. You can say you have faith in Jesus, but until you take a risk to follow him, you don't really have faith.

But what does this have to do with blood-stained pews? Everything.

Because faith *feels* like risk, every time you open up *feels* like a risk. You get the bubble guts. The Christian walk is a journey that never ends because there is always more faith to be had. When you first start following Christ, giving him 1 percent of your income may require all kinds of faith. Jesus will probably be amazed. But when you have been following him for years, giving a tithe that you're used to giving probably doesn't amaze him. You're comfortable: Why would that amaze Jesus? You'll probably have to give away 15 percent, 20 percent, or even 33 percent of your income to amaze Jesus. Faith always feels like risk.

And if our churches are going to be places of blood-stained pews, it means we must continually be taking risks.

Much of the time, in following Jesus, those risks are the things you hear about a lot—take a risk to read your Bible, take a risk to pray, take a risk to go on a mission trip or serve your local community. Yes, yes, yes, and yes. But the way we will experience true community is to take a risk in sharing with others, being open about our struggles, our stories, and our mess-ups.

I did jump off the faith pole, by the way. The people who were there have long since forgotten it because it didn't impact them. But here's what I can promise you: when you take a risk to initiate vulnerability, the people you are open with will not soon forget it, because they will have found the community they've been looking for.

———————————

A key to practicing vulnerability and embracing the awkward is going first. What if Ken Moore and Rob Wright had waited for a directive from up the command chain to use the church when they were dragging soldiers to safety? What if, at the first sign of opposition, they backed down? We wouldn't have the beautiful story we have today, and more importantly, soldiers wouldn't have had a safe place to bleed, be worked on, and be saved.

When you get the feeling that you know you need to be open, don't think of who will pull you down. Don't worry what could go wrong. Don't wait for permission. Just share. Choose to bleed. It's the only way you can get the help you so desperately need, whether that help is a simple prayer, counsel, or healing.

Apparently, there is something innate in all creatures that demands a challenge. John Ortberg describes it this way:

> Researchers at the University of California at Berkeley did an experiment some time ago that involved introducing an amoeba into a perfectly stress-free environment. Ideal temperature, optimal concentration of

moisture, constant food supply—the amoeba had an environment to which it had to make no adjustment whatsoever. So you would guess that that was one happy little amoeba. Whatever it is that gives amoebas ulcers and high blood pressure was gone. Yet, oddly enough, it died.[68]

We require change, adaptation, and challenge. Comfort alone will kill us. You can take a risk to be open and share, or you can take other, more self-destructive risks. But either way, you're going to take a risk, so it might as well be a risk that has the possibility of making you stronger, healthier, and more reliant on Jesus and others—a risk that also calls others to do the same.

The bottom line is, if I want to experience a community where people can bleed; if I want a community where the pews are stained with the blood of emotional, spiritual, and physical wounds; if I want a community where I can know and be known—I have to face the moment when I'd rather keep things on the surface and push my chips to the middle.

THE PRACTICE OF VULNERABILITY

Practicing vulnerability in church is the only way to build lasting and life-giving community. Through confession, living in community, living in truth, and taking a leap of faith, we will begin to participate in an openly broken community. It's messy, it's difficult, it's rarely straightforward, and it requires patience, faith, and grace—but I promise you it is beyond worth it.

We've been living without vulnerability, or with shallow versions of it, for far too long. It may take years to retrain your heart, mind, and soul to live this way. But do not give up, the hope is real, and the healing is on the horizon.

PART 3
MOVE
FORWARD

CHAPTER 10
MISSIONS: SHADOW AND CENTRAL

THE CHURCH EXISTS FOR NOTHING ELSE BUT TO DRAW MEN INTO CHRIST, TO MAKE THEM LITTLE CHRISTS. IF THEY ARE NOT DOING THAT, ALL THE CATHEDRALS, CLERGY, MISSIONS, SERMONS, EVEN THE BIBLE ITSELF, ARE SIMPLY A WASTE OF TIME. GOD BECAME MAN FOR NO OTHER PURPOSE.

—C.S. LEWIS

Earnest Shackleton wanted to be the first person to ever cross Antarctica. His team of twenty-seven men leave England aboard a ship called the *Endurance* in 1914. They sail but don't make it all the way to land because the ocean is freezing sooner than they'd anticipated. They get stuck in the ice, and after fighting it for many months, they eventually have to abandon ship as the ice crushes their boat.

Using lifeboats, they eventually row to the nearest land—Elephant Island—and set up camp. The only problem is that it is uninhabited. Shackleton sets off on one of the lifeboats with six other men, leaving the rest of his team behind, to attempt an 800-plus-mile journey across the open ocean in a lifeboat to the nearest place they knew was inhabited.

Seventeen days later, they reach the island of South Georgia. But they land on the wrong side of the island. From there, Shackleton and two others cross the mountains in the middle of the island. No one had ever crossed that land before.

They climb up and down mountains and glaciers, and thirty-six hours later, find the small sailing village. They are fed and cleaned. They go to the other side of the island, where they pick up the other three men who had been in the lifeboat with them. Finally, they make their way back to Elephant Island to pick up their crew and find that all twenty-two men they had left behind are still alive and healthy. Two years and a few weeks after starting their journey, they are all rescued and get to go home.[69]

How was Earnest Shackleton able to get a crew that didn't revolt, that didn't turn against each other, that was able to withstand the Antarctic winter even when things went horribly wrong? How did they make it through that hard time? These are the questions I pondered when I heard this story.

Earnest Shackleton's recruitment technique teaches us something important. If I was recruiting a crew to be the first people to ever cross Antarctica, the temptation would be to talk about glory and fame or maybe talk about how it could be fun and downplay the danger. But here's the advertisement Shackleton placed:

Men Wanted for Hazardous Journey. Small Wages, bitter cold, long months of complete darkness, constant

danger, safe return doubtful. Honour and recognition in case of success.

Legend has it that he couldn't keep up with all the applicants.[70]

The reason the church often fails to be a place of blood-stained pews is found in Earnest Shackleton's story, as well as in Moore and Wright's story: the mission has to be central.

Think of Ken Moore and Rob Wright: It's D-Day. They're going against one of the most evil dictators of all time in Hitler, trying to be forces of good in the face of evil. People are getting shot. War is in their face. What if, with bullets flying, Moore says to Wright, "You know, I don't really like this church's architecture; I think we should move the soldiers somewhere else." Or what if Wright responds, "This is hard work. I don't want to go find injured soldiers. I'll wait here in the church, and if they happen to come to me, then I'll help them." What if either of them said, "This isn't very much fun. Let's talk about a way to make this more fun for us, and then we can go find some injured soldiers." That would be absurd!

But how often do churches not help bleeding, broken people because the people in the church are focused on what we want to do instead of what God has called us to do?

Earnest Shackleton was on to something. When he needs a group of men to face treacherous conditions and possible death, he doesn't sugar-coat it. He doesn't try to make it sound like something it isn't. He just puts it out there: "This is hard and could result in death, but you will be a part of something amazing." And it reminds me of something Jesus said.

When Jesus first brings into being the idea of church, he says, "The gates of hell shall not prevail against it" (Matthew 16:18, ESV). At first glance that sounds like Jesus is saying that whatever attack came up on the church, the church would survive. I mean, he says the gates of hell won't "prevail." If I'm talking sports and say, "The Steelers will not prevail against my beloved Baltimore Ravens," I mean the Steelers will give their best shot, but the Ravens will withstand it and win.* But somewhere along the line, I was reminded of what I learned in high school history class.

In ancient cities, walls were the primary defense mechanism. And in a walled city, gates were the most vulnerable place to attack. If you attacked a city, you wouldn't attack the stone wall; you'd attack the gates and try to conquer the city that way.

So at the very first mention in history of this thing called the church, Jesus here is telling us, the *church* is the one on attack. The church is going to be attacking hell and hell *will not win*. Jesus is saying, "I have a mission for you. The mission will be hard. The mission will be a battle. The mission has eternal ramifications." At the very founding of the church, Jesus says the church *must* be on mission. And when the church is on mission, *that* is when small bickering goes away. That is when my personal preference is set aside. That is when we do what the church was meant to do.

Now that doesn't mean things are perfect, though. One of my friends said it to me this way: "The face of true unity looks like honesty. We often think unity is kindness, and it feels a little superficial; we avoid conflict or hard conversations. In part, unity is kindness, but deep down it is genuine honesty that then still chooses one another because Christ has chosen us." In other words, disagreement will happen and personal preference still exists, but the mission will be more important.

So far, I've shared multiple examples of the church acting dysfunctional. But there's one reason I have hope for the church: Jesus did. When man or woman tries to build the church, it doesn't work. But when Jesus

---

*You don't know how hard it was for me to put the word St**lers in my book. May God forgive me. Go Ravens. (And yes, I blotted it out like the cussword it is.)

leads the church, it is a "me too" community that is on mission. Moore and Wright were on a mission. Blood-stained pews happened because they knew the mission and they ran after it. They ran after the broken and the bleeding and they brought them in. So, let's clarify how God's mission inevitably leads to blood-stained pews.

GOD'S MISSION PUTS ME ON ATTACK

I'm not very good at video games, because I don't play them that often. But for my level of expertise, one thing I've figured out, that's true on most games, is I've got to attack. If I just hide in a cave or under the dock, I may not die, but I'm not going to accomplish anything. I have to get out from where I'm hiding, face the enemy, and attack with everything in me. Sure, I die sometimes. But then sometimes I succeed, and I never succeed if I just hide and try to protect myself.

This makes me think of a story from Westminster Abbey in London, one of the most famous churches in the world. It has hosted royal weddings and funerals; hundreds of famous people are buried there. Millions visit the church each year. Herschel Ford tells the story of a tour guide who proudly showed a group of tourists through Westminster Abbey, that grand cathedral. He "boasted about the ornate architecture, the expensive appointments," impressive history, and the famous people who had sat in the centuries-old pews. When he was finished, he asked the tourists, "'Are there any questions?' One plainly dressed, elderly woman said, 'Yes, sir. Has anyone been saved here lately?'"[71]

If Moore and Wright could take you on a tour of their setup, show you their medical supplies, explain the training they had done and that was the end of it, you'd look at them and say, "But wait a second, you guys are medics. Have you actually *saved* anyone?"

What matters for church is not the building. It's not the production. It's simply, has anyone been saved lately? That is God's mission. We're on attack.

GOD'S MISSION FOCUSES ON THE LOST

One of Jesus' most famous stories is in Luke 15: A dad has two sons. One of them says, "Dad, I wish you were dead. Give me my inheritance now." The dad acquiesces and the son does what any young punk who has the guts to say something like that would do: he parties the money away. When it's all gone and he's envious of what pigs eat, he decides to go home, tail between his legs. But his dad doesn't scold him. He doesn't make him do penance. He doesn't reject him. Instead, he throws a party. He says, "My son was lost and is found. He was dead and is alive. It's time to celebrate." He gets out the filet mignon that they've been saving for a special occasion (see Luke 15:11–32).

Maybe the most interesting part of this story is Jesus' audience. The chapter starts with this: "Tax collectors and other notorious sinners often came to listen to Jesus teach. This made the Pharisees and teachers of religious law complain that he was associating with such sinful people—even eating with them! So Jesus told them this story" (Luke 15:1–3). Jesus is making the point: understand the heart of God. His heart is for his lost kids.

I love the phrase "notorious sinners" the New Living Translation uses to describe the crowd that follows Jesus. It makes me appreciate even more the word "lost" that Jesus uses in Luke 15. Lost isn't a mean term. Lost doesn't mean you're the world's worst person. Lost doesn't mean you're stupid. Lost doesn't mean you're a project. Often, you're not even lost because you meant to be lost. Lost simply means you need help to get to the right destination. That's who Jesus came for, the lost. That is who God's heart beats for.

Several years ago, my wife and I were hanging out in our townhouse on a random Saturday. At the time, we had only two kids (now we have four), ages two years and six months. We were watching TV when my wife said, "Where's Reagan [the two-year-old]?" I didn't see her, so I went down to the first floor, but a quick glance said she wasn't there. I hollered up to Lindsay, "She's not down here." Lindsay said back, "But I know she didn't go upstairs."

That's when I noticed the front door was cracked open. I have to tell you that my first reaction was pride. I thought, *You better believe my two-year-old knows how to unlock and open doors! Genius!* But that proud smile quickly faded as I opened the door, walked outside, and didn't see Reagan. I hollered upstairs that Reagan had gone outside but I didn't see her. So, my wife scooped up the baby and headed one direction; I went the other.

My heart started beating fast. My palms were sweating. I had visions of stories I'd seen on the news. We didn't even know how long Reagan had been gone. When was the last time I saw her? Was it ten minutes ago? Twenty? It felt like an hour.

I was walking down the street, trying to stay calm, praying that she simply found a neighbor's tricycle, and I'll see her any minute. From down the street, I can hear that my wife is not keeping it as calm on the outside as I am, because I hear her screaming Reagan's name with a terror-filled tone that only the mother of a lost child can have. I'd never heard that tone in my wife's voice before then, and I've never heard it since.

By this time, I'd reached the end of the street and headed back home to get a bike, thinking I could cover more territory quicker. Lindsay also gave up at this point and ran back home to get her phone, preparing to call 911. Lindsay raced home, ran up to the second floor where her phone was in the kitchen, and as she reached down to grab her phone, she glanced through the blinds. About sixty houses down the street, there is a gap between townhouses. And there, walking by herself, is a little two-year-old with brown hair and a ponytail, having the time of her life. Lindsay drops the phone, races down the street, all the while carrying our six-month-old, Quint.

By the time Lindsay found her, Reagan had approached a dog that a neighbor was walking. She was hunched over, petting this dog, completely oblivious and having the time of her life in her newfound freedom. Lindsay ran up screaming her name, scooped her up, and started bawling. At this point, Reagan could tell something was wrong, so she started crying. Meanwhile, the neighbor was just staring at them, probably thinking our family was crazy.

Later, after my heart rate was normal again, and I could think with a clear head, I realized that day I got a small taste of what God feels like. See, here's a thought that never went through my head as we searched for Reagan: *At least we've got Quint.* I could've rationalized, "Why should I be greedy and want two kids? Some people close to me can't have any kids. Plus, Reagan's starting to get an attitude sometimes; this serves her right. That's what she gets for going outside when she shouldn't. She deserves this. I'll just keep Quint since he did what he was supposed to do, and Reagan can be on her own."

If I had thought that, I'd be the worst parent in history! But how often do we do that in church? If someone does something they're not supposed to or if they let us down, we say, "See you later," and write them off. But Jesus says no. I came for the lost. We're on a mission, and hell won't prevail.

And this isn't some philosophical thing for me. I've had people in church hurt *me*, let *me* down, and throw false accusations at me. When they got mad and left our church, what I wanted to say was, "Serves you right. See you later." But God's mission compels me to not give up, because God's heart is to run after his lost kids.

If Moore and Wright had only been around, or seen, healthy soldiers, they could've rightly assumed that they weren't needed. They could've gotten lazy, relaxed, and not contributed anything. It was only by going out and looking for the wounded that they could achieve their mission. We are no different.

I remember one time in the lobby of our church's building talking with a guy in our church. He had told me for months that the person he most wanted to accept Jesus was his brother. His brother had made some dumb decisions, wasn't a church person, and didn't show any interest in Jesus. But one day, this guy came up to me before church with a big grin on his face and said, "My brother's here!" I could tell it was kind of his way to tell me, "Don't screw up the sermon. You better be good tonight!"

I thought the sermon went well. After service I was in the lobby, where I spotted him. I went over to him and asked, "How'd your brother like it?" He opened his mouth to speak, but nothing came out. His lip quivered. His eyes welled up with tears. I could hear the heartbreak in his voice when he finally said, "He fell asleep." When he said that, I heard the ache in his voice that can only be uttered by someone who is praying relentlessly for the salvation of someone they love.

Let me ask you: When is the last time you cried over someone else's salvation? When is the last time you laid awake praying that someone would come to church with you so they could find hope? When is the last time that the worst part of your week was someone turning down your invite to church? When you are *that* connected to the lost, you are on God's mission. You are attacking hell itself. And in case you don't know, people who need that hope are all around you.

One time in our church, we did this exercise that was kind of hokey yet powerful. We have our baptism tub in the front of our auditorium and hearing the stories from that tub of why people are making Jesus their leader and forgiver forever is the best thing we get to be a part of. As a reminder that we are on God's mission, one week we gave everyone a ball and asked them to write down the name of someone they want to see give their life to Jesus. Then, during a song, everyone walked to the tub and dropped the ball in.

The next day, I was looking at those balls to see the names and pray over them, but I was shocked at the most common name that was written: "Me." Over and over and over people had written "me," "myself," even "me and my husband" as who they wanted to see give their lives to Jesus one day. It was a tangible reminder that there are lost people all around us; we just have to open our eyes to see them.

It's why I love Sam Shoemaker's famous poem. Sam was cofounder of Alcoholics Anonymous and he wrote this poem about being on mission with God:

> I stay near the door.
> I neither go too far in, nor stay too far out,
> The door is the most important door in the world—
> It is the door through which men walk when they find
> God.
> There's no use my going way inside, and staying there,
> When so many are still outside, and they, as much as I,
> Crave to know where the door is.
> I admire the people who go way in.
> But I wish they would not forget how it was
> Before they got in. Then they would be able to help
> The people who have not even found the door,
> Or the people who want to run away again from God....
> As for me, I shall take my old accustomed place,
> Near enough to God to hear Him, and know He is there,
> But not so far from men as not to hear them,
> And remember they are there too.
> Where? Outside the door—
> Thousands of them, millions of them.
> But—more important for me—
> One of them, two of them, ten of them,
> Whose hands I am intended to put on the latch,

So I shall stay by the door and wait
For those who seek it.
'I had rather be a door-keeper . . .'
So I stay near the door.[72]

GOD'S MISSION KEEPS US FOCUSED

Moore and Wright knew their mission was to help and heal injured soldiers. That drove them to keep going all night on D-Day. Jesus said we're
supposed to attack hell. If we keep that in mind, we will run to the lost,
hurting, broken, and bleeding. But if we lose that mission, we'll become
like the Church of God Grill.

The Church of God Grill is a restaurant in Atlanta, Georgia. But it
used to be a church. Every week after service, they would cook these big
chicken dinners and the proceeds would go to support the mission of
the church. But the food gained such prestige that they started cutting
the church service shorter. It kept being so popular that eventually they
shut down the church and just kept the restaurant open. The name never
changed, so today you can visit the Church of God Grill, even though
there's no church.[73]

What happened there? They forgot the mission of the church. While
most churches probably won't turn into restaurants, most Christians
tend to—over time—focus on things that don't matter and forget God's
mission to attack hell.

A few years ago, my family was spending a Saturday afternoon relax-
ing and watching college football; in the middle of the afternoon our
doorbell rang. We weren't expecting any company, so I didn't know who
would be ringing our doorbell. I opened the door to find two people
on our doorstep who were dressed nicely. They introduced themselves
and then asked me a question about the Bible. I looked across the street
and saw another couple ringing a doorbell and realized some church or

maybe even cult was canvassing our neighborhood. I enjoy a good Bible discussion, so I told them I'd love to talk to them.

They started off asking me a question about heaven. I answered with what the Bible says, and I could tell they were a little surprised I got the answer "right." I assumed they were going to use that to then ask something like, "Do you know you'll go to heaven when you die?" But instead, they took a left turn and started asking really obscure questions about finite pieces of theology regarding what our bodies will be like in heaven. During the entire conversation, I continued to give the biblical answers and they didn't seem to know what to say. It was obvious they were used to correcting people. Every time they would ask me a question, after my answer, the guy would say, "That's right, Carl. In the Bible the prophet Daniel says this." And he was pointing to these obscure Scriptures.

We talked for about ten minutes, and then they said, "Okay, thanks for your time. Have a good day!" They left, I shut the door, and I went upstairs. It was a pretty random experience, but as I reflected on it later, I couldn't believe what had happened. These people were going door to door in my neighborhood to convince people about a very obscure theology that doesn't really have any practical application. At the end of it, they never once talked about church—and more importantly, they never once talked about Jesus. In their effort to understand the Bible, they forgot what the Bible was all about. I was left shaking my head, thinking, *They are wasting their time!* But then God's Spirit matter-of-factly said, "Carl, are you any different?"

When people come to your church, do they deal with their anger but not meet Jesus? When people hear us share from Scripture, are they impressed by a good story or by Jesus? When people leave our churches, do they talk about our production or do they talk about Jesus?

The people who canvassed my neighborhood had great energy and passion, but it was misplaced. I respect their boldness because I haven't canvassed a neighborhood like that—I'd be too intimidated to ring random doorbells! But their passion wasn't driven by God's mission. How much more effective would those people have been if they were asking how they could pray for me? How much more attractive would their group have been if they'd told me Jesus came to give me rest instead of talking about obscure parts of Bible prophecy? They lost the mission, and in the process, they lost their effectiveness.

WARNING: SHADOW MISSIONS EXIST

Now I must warn you: you can get off track. A prompt that helps me figure out what I need to be open about, how I need to "bleed" in front of others, is this question: What is my shadow mission?

I first heard this phrase from John Ortberg, who says your shadow mission is to revolve your life around something trivial. Ortberg was at a retreat with some Christian leaders and one of the guys said his shadow mission was to watch porn while the world goes to hell. Everybody laughed. Then he said, "I'm going to say this one more time ... only this time, I want you to listen and not laugh. . . . 'My shadow mission is to watch TV and masturbate while the world goes to hell.'"[74]

So many people today want to figure out their purpose, but I believe it's maybe equally important to first define your shadow mission. What is your shadow mission? What is the thing that you can pour yourself into—even get some self-worth from and probably have fun doing it—but in the end is a shallow existence; it is *not* God's purpose for you?

God's purpose for you serves other people; your shadow mission serves yourself.

What's your shadow mission?

- Is it to watch porn while the world goes to hell?
- Is it to make as much money as you can so you can spend it all on yourself?

- Is it for *you* to have sexual satisfaction?
- Is it to get really good at video games?
- Is it to have a family that looks good in photos?
- Is it to rise up the corporate ladder and show that you've got what it takes?
- Is it to numb yourself by whatever means necessary?
- Is your shadow mission to read a lot of books to show people that you're intellectual?
- Is your shadow mission to get really good at your hobby?
- Is your shadow mission to look really good in front of the mirror?

What's your shadow mission? I'll tell you mine. My shadow mission is to lead a church that *looks* successful.

Here's what I mean: I want to lead a church that has good production and is engaging, looks good on social media while the charts of attendance, giving, and baptisms all go up and to the right. Here's the thing: I could achieve all that and still neglect the hard work of helping people practice spiritual disciplines and to love and live like Jesus. And I could neglect being open about *my* brokenness, which makes other people not be vulnerable. That means we could create a community where we lift up the name of Jesus but everyone hides their pain and hurt; where we don't really let Jesus heal us down deep so we never experience the true life he offers. But on the outside, everything would look great, so no one would rock the boat.

I'm like you in that I want to say, "Our church is definitely for the lost and the broken and the bleeding." But what I really mean—at least what my actions would indicate—is that I'm okay with you bleeding when you show up, but you better get well, and you better get well quickly if you want to stick around. I wouldn't say that out loud. If pressed I don't think I'd even admit that. But when I look at what agitates me about people over time in the church, it's this very thing, that they don't "get better" on my timeline.

See, the thing about a shadow mission is sometimes nobody else will know. Nobody else will know if you're pursuing a shadow mission or the purpose God made you for, because sometimes the difference is just the heart behind it or what happens behind closed doors.

Most of the time your shadow mission is the thing you passively fall into if you just live life by reacting to what happens to you. But when you put into words your shadow mission, it acknowledges what it is and shows that you have a choice between living full of purpose and just passively living your shadow mission. When you speak about it, it begins to lose its power. In fact, I challenge you today to text, call, or email someone right now to say, "I just need to get it out there. Here's my shadow mission." And then maybe explain the concept of shadow mission to them.

When your shadow mission starts consuming your time and energy, remind yourself of God's mission. Run after the lost, attack the gates of hell, bring people to God so they can experience his grace.

Cameron is a pastor, and one time the church he worked at had a woman who was pregnant with triplets. Everyone was excited for her, but that's a high-risk pregnancy, so many people were praying for her to see these triplets born healthy. Well, one day Cameron got the call: the triplets had been born. But there was a problem. The two boys were born healthy, and they were going to make it, but the little girl was brain-dead, and she was on a ventilator—she was not going to make it.

So, throughout the drive to the hospital, Cameron racked his brain about what to say, what Scripture to read, and what to pray. And he could never figure out the right words to comfort people going through such a unique time of both joy and grief. But he knew what he was not going to say. He was not going to stroll into that delivery room and say, "Why are you guys crying? You got two healthy babies. Many people can't even have children. Why are you so sad about this?" He knew if he uttered those words, the tear-stained face of a broken-hearted mother would look back at him, point to a baby girl on a ventilator, and say, "But I want that one too."

Jesus believes in hell. Don't miss that. But he came so we could have heaven. I don't think his main concern is how many seats are filled, what style of music is played, or how good the coffee is. I think he's looking at your neighbor, your coworker, the person who sits next to you at school, and he's pointing at them with the heartache only the father of a runaway child can have and saying, "I want that one too."

Jesus has called us to a great mission. The byproduct of this will be a church where it's safe to bleed, safe to be broken, safe to be open and real. But we will not experience that if we bow to personal preference, cater to insiders, or hang on to the past. It's time to attack the gates of hell.

CHAPTER 11
MOSAICS: FAKE AND REAL

PRETENTIOUSNESS REPELS BUT AUTHENTICITY ATTRACTS,
AND VULNERABILITY IS THE PATHWAY TO INTIMACY.

—RICK WARREN

If you do a quick internet search of "New York subway mosaics," you see some impressive artwork. It may simply be the name of the station, sometimes it's a sign, and occasionally it's an entire mural—but the intricacy involved in these mosaics is impressive and beautiful.

If you find yourself in Williamsburg in Brooklyn, you'll notice several beautiful mosaics reminding you what station you are in. If you look at the wall, you'll see a large one. If you look at the pillar on the platform, you'll see another—made of black and white tiles that have been there for decades, their cracks giving the station a unique character.

But if you look at another pillar, you'll see what at first glance looks like just another mosaic, saying, "Morgan Ave." Upon closer inspection, however, you'll notice that it's in fact *not* a mosaic at all. Rather, it's a plastic sign that was printed to *look* like a mosaic. If you're far away, you can't even tell the difference. But when you get close you realize, "Oh, this sign is supposed to *look* like it's made of broken pieces, but it's actually clean, shiny and neat."

And this is the exact temptation you will face with the church. The church is a mosaic. It is made up of broken people that the world would look at and say, "You're not worth very much." But like the artist he is, God takes the broken pieces of our lives and forms us together into something beautiful that he calls the church. But the temptation is to say. "I *was* broken." The temptation is to *look* broken. The temptation is to *pretend* to be broken.

This is why it's so important to have the inward posture of vulnerability as you practice vulnerability in the context of community. You must be consistent in your pursuit of vulnerability, being endlessly honest with yourself and others when masks or pretenses get in the way of true vulnerability. What we're talking about is consistency of vulnerability.

The reason is, we will always be drawn back toward being fake, toward hiding, toward wearing masks.

A principal of physical growth relates to the spiritual growth we're talking about here. The principle law of adaptation is called SAID—the law of Specific Adaptation to Imposed Demands.[75] In essence, SAID says that the body will only adapt to the minimum possible amount to overcome any particular challenge. And once your body adapts, it will continually look for more efficient ways to perform the task at hand. The principle of SAID explains why you need to consistently change your workouts to shock your body into getting healthier and healthier.

But I find this is also true with vulnerability. When you first choose to be vulnerable, sharing a small dream will feel like a big risk, but in time you will be comfortable sharing that thing. Then you will have to share a new thing. Then you will share a new thing after that. It's difficult because the journey ever ends.

The bad thing about that church in Angoville is that today that church is a museum to the past. When a church body focuses more on what they did in the past than how they can help the bleeding in the present, it ceases to be what Jesus dreamed of when he said, "The gates of hell will not overcome it." The church in Angoville-au-Plain is a great tourist site. It's a moving experience. It's a tribute to those who fought and died for freedom. But that's all it is. It no longer helps those who are bleeding. It no longer helps the broken and wounded.

It seems a lot of churches these days are museums to the past: museums to old kinds of music, old styles of ministry, old cultural moments etched in time. They proudly display the name of "church," but if you're looking for somewhere to go when you are bleeding, you're in the wrong place.

I love college basketball, specifically watching the team from where I grew up: the University of Louisville. When I moved a third of the way across the country for my first job out of college, I remember seeing a guy with a Louisville basketball T-shirt on during my first week. I excitedly ran up to him and started talking all things Louisville basketball, thinking I had just met my new best friend. He smiled and listened, but when I said, "We should get together to watch a game on TV," he said, "Oh, I don't watch games. I just like the shirt because I used to live there." I was crushed! He went from my new best friend to a complete loser in my eyes in a moment, because he advertised that he was a fan, but the reality was something different. That's what so many churches do today—they call themselves churches but are not safe places for the bleeding and broken.

True vulnerability isn't like that Morgan Ave mosaic: it's real, it's gritty, it's broken, it's messy, but it's the most life-giving thing you'll ever experience. Together, as a church, all our broken pieces build a mosaic of restoration, redemption, and grace that cannot be rivaled. When *that* happens, you are truly part of the church—not a "fake mosaic" type of church, but a church full of broken people, held together by a perfect God, expressing itself through patient, genuine love.

————————————

You may be thinking, *Carl, you talk a lot about vulnerability. But this and the previous chapter seem to be a right turn onto what the corporate church is supposed to be. What's the connection?*

Here's the connection: the only thing keeping the church on mission is you. The only thing keeping the church real is you. It's not on a pastor. It's not on a seasoned believer. It's not on the next generation to get it right. It's on you. When *you* are openly broken, you will keep the church on mission.

Let me remind you: the church is not a building, program, or celebrity pastor. The church is people. *You* are the church. The way *you* choose to live out vulnerability will determine if the church is a real mosaic or a fake mosaic.

In fact, let me take you to Jesus' story to remind you that this has always been true.

FAMILY TREE

When you're writing a book, a lot of people will tell you, "You've got to get the first sentence right. That'll make or break you." It seems a little dramatic, but I get it. And if you're still reading, apparently you thought mine was good enough (or you're a family member). This piece of advice, however, was something that apparently no one told Matthew.

Matthew wrote the first Gospel of the New Testament. It tells the story of Jesus and begins the story of God after a four-hundred-year period of silence. It contains Jesus' most famous sermon, many great teachings and miracles, and of course, the story of his death and resurrection. You'd think it would start off with a bang, maybe like some of the greatest stories of all time. But the way this book starts is, well, *not too exciting* would be an understatement: "This is a record of the ancestors of Jesus the Messiah, a descendant of David and of Abraham" (Matthew 1:1). It doesn't get much better from there, either: "Abraham was the father of Isaac. Isaac was the father of Jacob. Jacob was the father of Judah and his brothers" (Matthew 1:2).

And it just goes on and on and on. There are forty-eight names total in the genealogy of Matthew chapter one. And while it can be boring to read, and I'm sure it carries an important weight for the original readers of this Gospel, it contains a couple important details that are important for us too. There are several inserted notes, unnecessary for a simple genealogy, that show us who God came for.

The first note comes in verse three where Matthew tells us that Tamar is the mother of Perez and Zerah. This doesn't seem like a big deal unless you know the story, because the story is crazy: Judah's son marries Tamar, but then is struck down by God because of his wickedness (see Genesis 38). They had no children, and having no children was both a social slap in the face and hurt economically. In the days before government welfare, your children cared for you in your old age. Therefore, no children meant no one to feed you. So long story short, if a man died, his brothers had to provide an heir for their sister-in-law.

Tamar complains to her father-in-law, Judah, that he needs to help her get a child. He does nothing. So, she takes the drastic step and disguises herself as a prostitute. Then she has sex with Judah, her father-in-law. She apparently has a veil on the whole time or they are in complete darkness because he doesn't realize who he had sex with. Months later, he finds out Tamar is pregnant even though she's not married, and he calls for her to be executed, but she sends him a message to basically say, "Hey father-in-law, you're the father of this baby!"

This story raises about fifty questions. And to be clear, the Scriptures don't include this to say this is what you *should* go out and do, but to say, "Here's what happened." Matthew goes out of his way as he begins his Gospel to say, "Remember that reality TV episode in our lineage? Yeah, Jesus came from that."

A few names later we read, "Boaz was the father of Obed (whose mother was Ruth)" (Matthew 1:5). There's nothing too crazy here, unless you know that ancient Jews were very particular about their lineage, and they weren't supposed to marry outside their people. Ruth is a foreigner. She isn't Jewish. But Matthew says, "Hey, don't forget about that outsider who married into our people. Jesus came from her, too."

The last one I want to point out is in verse 6: "David was the father of Solomon (whose mother was Bathsheba)." This is probably the biggest screw-up in the history of the Jewish people, because David is their most famous king. He is described as a man after God's own heart. He brings peace. He funds their temple. He writes more psalms than anyone else in the Old Testament. But he has an affair with Bathsheba and tries to cover it up. Matthew describes Bathsheba as "the widow of Uriah." That doesn't sound too bad, until you remember that the reason she is a widow is because David had her husband killed so he could marry her. David thinks he has covered everything up until God's prophet brings it all to light, and the entire country becomes aware that their king murdered someone just so he could marry his wife—who he'd already slept with. This is one of the black eyes of Israel's history, so in opening up the story about Jesus Matthew says, "Don't forget that really bad thing that happened: Jesus came from that, too."

As he opens his Gospel, Matthew goes out of his way to remind the reader of how treacherous, shameful, and downright ugly their history and specifically Jesus' line is. Why? Because he wants to show who Jesus came *from* and who Jesus came *for*. Let's look at Jesus' words in Matthew 11:28–30 (MSG) again:

Are you tired? Worn out? Burned out on religion? Come
to me. Get away with me and you'll recover your life.
I'll show you how to take a real rest. Walk with me and
work with me—watch how I do it. Learn the unforced
rhythms of grace. I won't lay anything heavy or ill-fitting
on you. Keep company with me and you'll learn to live
freely and lightly.

That's it, folks. That's who Jesus came for. Another translation says
he came for those who are weary with heavy burdens. Jesus came to give
you peace. He came to relieve your suffering. He came to bring a hope
that cannot fade away. He came to bring you through church doors to
find a place of belonging and grace.

Make no mistake: the church was never meant to be a club for the
healthy or a gathering for the perfect; the church was never meant to be
a show, a production, a carrier of tradition, or a membership club. The
church was not started to achieve political gain or business influence.
What Kenneth Moore and Robert Wright saw on D-Day at a thousand-
year-old church is what it was always intended to be: a place of blood-
stained pews, a place for the broken and burdened, a place for all of us.

––––––––––

Several years ago, I had just finished preaching at our Saturday night
service and was standing in the lobby after to say hi to folks as I always
do. I was having the typical conversations—someone needed prayer,
someone wanted to say hello, another person wanted to talk sports. But
the whole time, I could see this guy I didn't recognize hanging out in
the back of the group waiting to talk to me. He looked uncomfortable. I
didn't recognize him, but I kept looking at him because he looked agi-
tated and, frankly, like life had beaten him up a little. He just looked tired.

Finally, most of the people had cleared out and this guy made his way up to me. He had anger on his face, with a clenched jaw, weathered skin, and a hard brow. I introduced myself and asked, "What can I do for you?" He looked at me with a frank honesty that most lobby conversations at church lack and demanded, "What in the hell in that sermon was for me?" His honesty was a jolt of ice water thrown on me and didn't quite square with all the "nice sermon" comments I was used to getting.

But in three seconds I was able to put this story together. I could see physically what was true in his soul. He'd had a rough life. He was beaten down. He had metaphorically crawled into our little warehouse building that night, hoping against hope he'd find something he could cling to, some glimmer of possibility that things could get better for him. For some reason he thought, *Maybe church can help*.

And as I quickly recalled the main points of my sermon, I realized it had been a great sermon—if your life was already together. It had been a great sermon—if you already loved Jesus and had a family and just needed a couple encouraging anecdotes to lift your already-high spirits. But for the truly broken, for the truly hopeless, it didn't add much. It didn't have grace throughout. It didn't encourage anyone to bleed in our pews. It didn't communicate to this broken shell of a man that hope is for everyone. So, I looked him in the eye and honestly said, "Nothing. Nothing was for you. And I'm sorry." He left and I never saw him again.

To those of you who gave up on church because it was irrelevant or there were too many people wearing masks, I'm sorry. I'm sorry for when we let our idea of a cool program get in the way of preaching hope. I'm sorry for when I cared more about sounding like a polished public speaker than I did helping hurting people get hope. I'm sorry for when I didn't communicate it was safe to bleed, because I feared bleeding in front of people. I'm sorry for when social media rants seemed to communicate that Christians cared more about a political party than being a hospital for the broken. I'm sorry that we've focused on keeping our triage center clean instead of finding bleeding people to bring in.

HOW LOST IS TOO LOST?

I saw some jeans for sale not too long ago from a high-end department store that were labeled "heavily distressed jeans." They were sold to look like they were muddy! And catch this: the price tag was a mere $425. You could pay four Benjamins to look like your jeans were muddy. And in case you're wondering, you can wash these jeans, and they maintain the muddy look.

Think about these jeans though. You put them on when you want to look like you've put in a hard day's work but all you did was go to a department store. Moore and Wright didn't take a little vial of blood and sprinkle it on some pews on D-Day to create a cool image. People bled. People died. People suffered. That's how you get a church with blood-stained pews.

Here's a question that gets to the point: In your church, how lost is *too* lost? Is your church for alcoholics, really? Because if your church is for alcoholics, you know what you will smell on people in the church? Alcohol. Have you sat in a church service where the main thing you noticed wasn't the good song or the Scriptural insight, but the smell of the person sitting next to you and you wondered if they were sober enough to get anything out of what was happening?

Is your church for prostitutes? Really? Some of the prostitutes I've encountered don't have good boundaries when it comes to how they dress and how they interact with men. Have you sat next to a prostitute in church whose skirt was a little too short and who smiled a little uncomfortably at you?

Is your church for the child-obsessed mom? Really? One of Satan's best tricks is to turn a good thing into an ultimate thing, a false god if you will. Is your church a safe place for moms to say out loud, "The plan I have for my kid is 'X' and right now I don't really care what Jesus says about that"?

Is your church for the glutton? We have an obesity crisis in our country. Is the church a place where those people can come who neglect their bodies and say, "I just want to eat. Maybe it's to mask pain, maybe it's to feel good, maybe it's because I'm lazy. But that's what I do, it's who I am, and I don't think you can change me."

Is your church for the greedy? Have you seen people in church who put on a show of how good they look, how nicely they dress, how expensive their car is? Does your church welcome people who sometimes show up just to show an image?

You know what all these people have in common? They're all bleeding. They need a medic to fix them, but for that to happen, they need a pew on which they can bleed.

God started his church as the community where no matter what you've done, what you haven't done, who you've let down, or what shame you carry—you are welcome. You are sought after. You were bought. You are forgiven. And you've been placed in a community with other people like you, who are just trying to lean on the grace of Jesus to get them through another day.

GETTING STARTED

As you look inward, embrace the awkward, and move forward in this journey called vulnerability, remember to center Jesus' grace and redemption. Starting the journey of being openly broken in our lives and communities may feel overwhelming, so here's a statement to get you started on this journey of vulnerability, of bleeding in front of others. This is an exercise I learned from men I trust, and it has served me well. You get around a person or group that you are willing to bleed in front of—your crew—and you fill in this statement:

The truth I don't want you to know about me is

_____.

I've heard men fill in the blank with details about sexual sin. I've heard people confess adultery. I've heard dreams shared that had never been said out loud. It's a tough statement. It probably makes your palms sweat. But whatever it is that you would put in that blank is the reason you can say with Paul and the tax collector, "God, have mercy on me, a sinner."

One great moment relating to this phrase was something my friend Jonathan preached in our church once. He pulled up a picture of himself when he was in his twenties, also preaching at our church. We laughed at his hair and outfit and the bad stage design. But while he was showing this picture he talked about this phrase, "the truth I don't want you to know about me." And he talked about some embarrassing things from his past. But then he said, "That's actually not the truth I don't want you to know. That stuff is easy." After a pause he continued, "The truth I don't want you to know about me is, I spent more time picking out the outfit in this picture than praying that God's Word would affect you through that message."

"The truth I don't want you to know about me" could possibly be something dramatic or illegal. But it almost certainly is something that in your shame you want to hide—because it reveals your true character. Jonathan reminded me in that moment that vulnerability isn't about the weight of the thing I'm sharing as perceived by others; it's about what that thing is doing to me. The problem is it's not a onetime deal.

I've shared "the truth I don't want you to know about me" before. So, when I was asked to model this exercise on a recent men's retreat, I thought, *No problem, I've shared that before.* But before I could get too comfortable the leader dropped this bomb: "And remember, this isn't 'the truth I didn't want you to know six months ago.' This is 'the truth I don't want you to know today.'" Immediately I felt queasy, because once again I was faced with a choice of wearing a mask or choosing vulnerability and bleeding in front of others.

See, it's not enough to bleed once, because life involves pain. Life brings heartache. Life can be dull and disappointing. And life's not a trip; it's a journey. A church with blood-stained pews doesn't happen by accident. It happens when someone chooses to overcome their fast heart rate, lump in the throat, dry mouth, and once again say, "The truth I don't want you to know about me is," and gives an honest answer.

A fake mosaic can look good from a distance, but up close it looks cheap and lazy. Be a real mosaic. Be truly broken, with God filling in the gaps with the gold of his grace so you can be a beacon of hope to show others where to go to find eternal hope.

CHAPTER 12
OUTCASTS

THE PRIVILEGE OF A LIFETIME IS TO BECOME WHO YOU TRULY ARE.
—CARL JUNG

The past few years there have been many stories in the news about parents who give their kids idiotic names.

- A couple in Israel was inspired by the button on Facebook, so they named their child "Like."[76]
- Rob Morrow named his child "Tu"— as in to-morrow.[77]
- Ryan and Jami Hawkins, residents of Goshen, Indiana, put up the naming rights to their child on eBay back in 2004.[78]
- According to ABC News, there are three kids in the United States who bear the name "ESPN."[79]
- In Germany it is illegal to name your son (or your daughter) "Adolf Hitler" or "Osama bin Laden," which means someone had tried to do that.[80]
- In 2009, a New Jersey couple lost custody of their son "Adolf Hitler."[81]

Lindsay and I went to visit some friends in the hospital several years ago when they had a boy. We asked what his name was, and the dad said, "We don't know yet." And we asked what he meant, and he replied, "We're not sure what he looks like." I wanted to say, "He looks like a baby!"

Naming a kid is a big deal. Names can tell you a lot about a person—or at least their parents. I hope these presumably traumatized kids listed above changed their names. Names can be memorable in a way that gets you bullied or makes you famous. Many celebrities change their name for just that reason.

- Lady Gaga was first known as Stefani Joanne Angelina Germanotta. That's a mouthful.
- Chuck Norris was Carlos Ray.
- Elton John was born as Reginald Kenneth Dwight.
- Jamie Foxx's parents named him Eric Bishop.
- Muhammad Ali was originally Cassius Clay.
- And Alicia Keys was Alicia Augello Cook. (See what she did there?)

Names are a big deal. Because of that, you will often see individuals and groups in the Bible refer to God by a unique name that represents how he interacted with that person or group. Someone called God "Jehovah Jireh," which means "You're the God who provides." Jesus is called Emmanuél, which means "God is with us now." When I was doing my daily Bible reading recently, I came across a name for God I'd never noticed before. In Hebrew, it looks like this:

$$\text{יַחְדָּו צְבָקֶם הֹוהְי יָנֹדָא}$$

You pronounce it like this: Adonai Yehovah Kowvatz Nehdach. And here's how it translates in English: The Lord God Who Brings Back the Outcasts.

It was one of those moments you have every so often reading the Bible where you get chills and realize, God put this in here for me. As soon as I read it, I thought, *That's* me. *That's* us. *That's the* church. We worship the Lord God who brings back people like us. The reason I wrote this book is that God came for people like you and me. God came for misfits.

> The church is a bunch of misfits.
> In our seats are prostitutes and the people who use them.
> We have people addicted to porn, oxy, alcohol, and heroin.
> We have moms whose god is their children and dads whose god is their job.
> We have people who starve themselves and people whose go-to is gluttony.
> We have people who spend more time looking at social media in a day than they do hanging with friends in a month.
> We have marriage problems and kids who aren't healthy.
> We have intellectual doubts about the gospel and emotional triggers to Christians.
> But we're part of the church because when we look at Jesus we say, "Where else can we go?"

And I love being part of the church because the church is where I fit.

Am I the only one whose life feels like I'm on an emotional roller coaster?

Am I the only one who gets set off by small, seemingly trivial things?

Am I the only one who has dark thoughts?

Am I the only one who feels like a failure as a parent?

Am I the only one who feels like I have good friends, and then they do something that makes you not just ask who they are, but makes you feel stupid that you thought you were good friends in the first place?

Am I the only one whose life is still controlled by the scared, lonely kid inside?

Am I the only one who's just tired of everything?

Am I the only one who hears the promises of heaven and wants to say, "Let's get on with it already"?

I am the worst of sinners. I have shame and secrets and scars. And I need a community that says, "Me too." That's what I've found in the church.

At a recent church service, I included the name "The Lord God Who Brings Back the Outcasts" as part of my message. One of the people in the crowd that night was the brother of a friend of mine. They are, to put it mildly, estranged. He's made destructive choices and burned bridges. But my friend invited him to church. He said he'd show up at the 1:00 p.m. service but didn't show. Then he said he'd be there at 3:00 p.m. but didn't show. Five p.m. told the same story. Keep in mind that my friend was coming to every service because her brother kept saying he'd be there! Finally, at 7:00 p.m. he actually showed up, sat in the second row, and even seemed to pay attention.

After the service where I talked about the name "The Lord God Who Brings Back the Outcasts," my friend asked her brother, "What'd you think of the service?" His eyes started filling with tears. He rolled up his sleeve and showed her the homemade tattoo he'd gotten in prison. It simply said, "Outcast."

"I never thought I fit anywhere," he said. "Now I know I fit in the church, because God came for me."

God came for you. He takes you with all your cracks, broken pieces, failed dreams, and evil sins, and he gives you grace. He then places you in a community called the church, where it is safe to bleed, so he can mend you with the gold of his grace.

May a 900-year-old church building in Angoville, France, be our reminder that church is a place for people like us, people who are bleeding and need help. May we be the ones to initiate and to be vulnerable so that all our churches may be places with blood-stained pews, where being openly broken is celebrated, and where people are encouraged to live freely and lightly.

REACH OUT TO ME

I'd love to hear how this labor of love impacted you. Email me at carl@mosaicchristian.org to tell me your BSP story.

I love hearing feedback from my readers. Please leave me your thoughts and tell others what you enjoyed about *Blood Stained Pews*. You can scan the QR code below to leave a review on the Amazon book listing. Thanks!

ACKNOWLEDGMENTS

Thank you most of all to Lindsay for telling me on a train ride from Bayeux to Paris, "You need to write this book." You believe in me more than anyone, and your verbal and emotional encouragement breathes life into me. Doing life with you is the best.

Thank you, Mom, for encouraging me to write. You are the best encourager I know.

Thank you, Sarah, for making this project a priority amid everything else you do.

Thank you, Beth Ann, for always helping when needed.

Thank you, Amanda, for championing this project.

Thank you, Mosaic, for modeling what this book is about. It sounds good on paper, but you are the ones who've lived it for thirteen years and counting. Keep going.

Thank you to my staff for believing in me and following, even when I'm not sure where I'm headed. The way you model tenacious humility is inspiring.

Thank you to the Mosaic elders for believing in this project and making sure it's done well and done with integrity. You men are a gift of God.

Thank you, Philip Yancey, for teaching me the impact of the written word. You challenge and inspire me.

Thank you, Jim Burgen, for showing me grace during my brokenness as a teenager. You and your wife made sacrifices. It was worth it.

DISCUSSION GUIDE

INTRODUCTION | BLOOD-STAINED PEWS

1. When you think of the idea of a church having blood-stained pews, what comes to mind? What emotion do you feel?
2. Read again Jesus' quote:

   > Are you tired? Worn out? Burned out on religion? Come to me. Get away with me and you'll recover your life. I'll show you how to take a real rest. Walk with me and work with me—watch how I do it. Learn the unforced rhythms of grace. I won't lay anything heavy or ill-fitting on you. Keep company with me and you'll learn to live freely and lightly. (Matthew 11:28-30, MSG)

3. What is your response to that?
4. Philip Yancey said the author's experience is not the norm in the average church. Why do you think this is true (or not)?
5. What has your experience in the church been?
6. Take a moment to dream of what the church could be. What do you desire in true Christian community?

Own Your Growth:
Write a letter to a person who has given you hope for what the church could be. Don't have that person? Write a letter to yourself, to be read in one year, thanking yourself for doing the work to help build the church of your dreams.

CHAPTER 1 | LOOK IN THE MIRROR

1. When is the last time you got a case of the wells and made an excuse based on you being the exception? Was it to get out of a ticket? To get out of waiting in line? To get out of putting the kids to bed?

2. How would you explain the Fundamental Attribution Error in your own words?

3. Do you fall for the Fundamental Attribution Error? In what area of your life do you hold other people to a certain standard but exempt yourself from that same standard?

4. Read Luke 18:9-14. When was a time you prayed a prayer like this Pharisee?

5. Now think of it the other way: what would your life look like if you stopped holding others to unrealistic standards and, instead, took responsibility for yourself?

6. The author says we can view spiritual growth as a trip with a destination or as a journey of which we never fully arrive, this side of heaven. How do you fall into the trap of viewing spiritual growth as a trip? Are there areas where you think you have arrived?

7. Where have you been trying to forgive yourself? How does the explanation in this chapter release you from guilt and shame? How would your life change if you accepted Jesus' payment for your debt instead?

Own Your Growth:
This week write down the specific sin or broad area for which you've been trying to forgive yourself. Once you have prayed over that area of sin, burn it as you mentally hand it over to God and fully accept his forgiveness for it.

CHAPTER 2 | SLUMPED SHOULDERS

1. One of the footnotes discusses how the author's accent seemingly caused a problem for a woman he'd just met. Has your accent ever gotten you in trouble? What is your region famous for when it comes to accents or unique phrases/pronunciations?

2. In this chapter, we learned that shame is when you feel small. When is the first time you remember ever feeling shame?

3. Read again the comparison list of guilt vs. shame. Which do you tend to live in?

4. Sometimes shame sneaks into one area of our life more than others. What area of your life is that for you?

5. Read the full account of Peter's restoration in John 21:1-19. What emotions do you think Peter felt throughout his encounter with Jesus here?

6. The chapter ends by explaining that there is a difference between what we did (or what was done to us) and who we are. Where are you living like what you did, or do, is who you are?

> **Own Your Growth:**
> This week, begin each day by reading Matthew 3:17, and then spend a couple of moments in prayer. Be reminded that you are his dearly loved child who brings him great joy.

CHAPTER 3 | YOU HAVE HAD A HEART ATTACK

1. There are two types of people in the world: those who call the doctor when they're sick, and those who call Google. Which type are you? If you go to the self-diagnostic websites, what's the craziest fake diagnosis you ever assumed?

2. Read John 5:1-9. Carl wondered if the man's family dropped him off each morning. What other questions pop into your head as you read this story?

3. It may seem that Jesus is initially insensitive toward this man because he chooses not to heal him immediately. What is your reaction to Jesus' penetrating question "Would you like to get well?"

4. Is there an area of your life about which Jesus would ask the same question? How would you answer?

5. Carl said the lie he tells himself is that he gives 100 percent effort. What lie do you enjoy telling yourself?

6. If you have previously faced apathy and overcome it, how did you diagnose it and then deal with it?

> **Own Your Growth:**
> Jesus commanded the man in the story to walk, so you should do the same. Go on a 30-minute walk this week with no screens, music, or other people. As you walk, focus on Jesus' words, "Would you like to get well?" Pray to him about the lie you enjoy believing, repent of it, and ask him to make you well.

CHAPTER 4 | THE BEST PRAYER EVER

1. Read again John Ortberg's quote about doubt. Is this how you were taught to believe about faith in God? Describe that background.

2. What pain in and around you makes you ask questions of God?

3. Read Mark 9:14-29. Notice Jesus' words in verses 19 and 23. He almost sounds annoyed with the crowd yet still heals the man's son. What does this teach us about the character of Jesus?

4. Carl says we need to be real with God in three areas: disappointment, desires, and distress. Which one of these areas is easiest for you to talk to God about? Hardest? Why do you think that's true?

5. The chapter concludes with what Carl calls "the best prayer ever." Have you ever prayed this prayer and found it helpful?

Own Your Growth:
Think of a specific situation, relationship, or sin you've been struggling with. Pray the Best Prayer Ever over that situation every day this week.

CHAPTER 5 | WAX ON, WAX OFF

1. Share an awkward moment you've witnessed or been a part of recently.

2. We read the story of ancient Roman potters using wax to cover imperfections. Have you ever bought something that looked good only to find out it was a sham?

3. Expanding on the last question, have you ever felt that way about the church? Why?

4. Read Mark 3:1-6. After such a great miracle, the Pharisees plot how to kill Jesus. How do you think someone gets to this point? Maybe a more personal way to ask is this, if you were one of those Pharisees, what would have to be true to get to the point of wanting to execute Jesus?

5. What self-improvement plan or DIY project have you ever given up on because you couldn't do it perfectly? Why do we do that to ourselves?

6. We read, "Church is the worst form of community . . . except for every other form that has been tried." What makes you agree or disagree with that statement?

> **Own Your Growth:**
> Find a picture online of kintsugi, print it, and put it in a place where you will see it every day this week. When you see it, pray that God will help you be real about your brokenness.

CHAPTER 6 | BEATING UP BURGLARS

1. Re-read the list of reasons we keep secrets. Which of these reasons resonated the most with you and why?

2. The author argues that to "act like a Christian" typically means to have it all together but it *should* mean to simply act in a way that openly shows you need grace. Do you agree with that assessment? If so, have you heard that phrase ("act like a Christian") used as a weapon? How can you seek to redeem it?

3. Read Luke 12:1-3. What emotion does this elicit in you? Does it scare you? Excite you? Something else?

4. Think of when someone asked, "Can I be honest with you?" Was it really code for "Can I be open with you?" Why do you think we confuse honesty and openness?

5. Carl says we should confess the small stuff, the ridiculous dreams, and the dark stuff. They all have their own challenges. Which one is most difficult for you to bring to light? Why?

Own Your Growth:

Write your own PostSecret: on a postcard write out what your secret is. But don't keep it anonymous; mail it or text a picture of it to someone you trust, as an act of bringing it into the light.

CHAPTER 7 | FIND YOUR CREW

1. What is your favorite reality TV show?

2. Read Luke 6:12-16. What is your reaction to the fact that Jesus didn't choose to include *all* his disciples in his inner circle of 12?

3. Carl says to start slowly in building your crew. In your past, what happens when someone wants to become best friends too quickly?

4. Jim Burgen says to tell stories before they have bows on them. Have you had someone close to you live this out? What do their relationships typically look like? Have you found that you experienced closeness to them as a result?

5. Has your crew ever called you out? Describe how it was hard to hear but beneficial in the long run.

Own Your Growth:

Write down a list of who is in your crew of 3 and community of 12. Becoming aware of who those people are will help you to invest in them in the right ways. If you can't build this list, reach out to one person this week to begin the slow process of building your crew.

CHAPTER 8 | I NEED TO KNOW HOW TO DANCE

1. What is a funny truth you knew someone needed to hear but you were scared to tell them? Think food on their face, etc.
2. Read John 8:31-32 and John 14:6. Why are these profound statements of Jesus sometimes so difficult to believe?
3. Is there an area of your life or a specific circumstance where God's truth has been helpful?
4. Is it more difficult for you to believe God's truth is helpful, relevant, or eternal? What in your life makes you give that answer?
5. Do you have an "acceptable" sin—a sin that you rationalize is okay, when, in reality, God's truth says it is simply—sin?
6. What is your off-limits area for God's truth?

Own Your Growth:
What is the truth from God's Word you've been ignoring but that you need to accept and live in? Prayerfully figure that out and share it with someone who will cheer you on, as you take steps to change.

CHAPTER 9 | LEAP OF FAITH

1. Carl shared about great leadership from *Band of Brothers*. Who is a good example—real or fiction—of a great leader who goes first?

2. Read Mark 10:35-45. What seems pettiest in this story: James and John's request, the other disciples arguing, or something else?

3. The author said Jesus made himself vulnerable by becoming human and offering himself up as a sacrifice through his death. What aspect of Jesus' life and death do you think was the most vulnerable thing he did?

4. Carl challenges us to just share *something*. Often, we don't share because we over-analyze our thoughts, over-think our words, and over-stress ourselves about it. Why do we fall into this trap? How can we get out of it?

5. Can you think of a time when sharing something vulnerable felt like jumping into midair, hoping someone would catch the ropes you were attached to? Try to think less about what you shared and more about your emotion as you shared them. What made it so difficult?

6. Amoebas die in stress-free environments. Where do you see that same principle experienced in your life as it relates to vulnerability?

Own Your Growth:
The homework for chapter 7 was to make a list of your crew. This week your homework is to initiate a vulnerable conversation with them, inspired by this chapter.

CHAPTER 10 | MISSIONS: SHADOW AND CENTRAL

1. Legend says Ernest Shackleton recruited men with an ad promoting danger. Have you ever been attracted to a trip, mission, or team because it was advertised as being difficult?

2. Read Matthew 16:13-18. Did Carl's explanation provide a new understanding for you? Based on what you've read in this book, how does the church attack the gates of hell?

3. What is the most valuable thing you have ever lost? What would it mean for you to get it back?

4. Have you ever met a Christian who was so focused on a minute detail of the Bible that he/she missed the bigger picture? What was that like? Have *you* ever been that Christian?

5. Your shadow mission will distract you from God's mission for your life. Have you figured out what your shadow mission is? If not, who in your life could you ask to help you discern it?

Own Your Growth:

What is your shadow mission? Regardless of whether you normally journal or not, write a journal entry to God telling him about your shadow mission—what it is, how it is not on his mission, and why it is so sinister.

CHAPTER 11 | MOSAICS: FAKE AND REAL

1. The chapter opens by talking about a fake mosaic. Have you ever been tricked by something you thought was real only to find out later it was a fake?

2. Take a look at Matthew 1:1-17. Without any context, this section of Scripture seems dry and pointless. But knowing what Carl said, as well as other biblical background information, why is this opening to Jesus' story so striking?

3. Carl asks, how lost is too lost? Be honest—what situation, person, or sin background has ever made you uncomfortable in church?

4. Have you ever been like the guy in Carl's story who came to church only to find nothing for his pain? How did that experience affect you?

5. Was there ever a truth that at one point you didn't want people to know, but once you got it out, it lost its power?

Own Your Growth:
Commit to telling one person this week "the truth I don't want you to know." Yes, you flexed this muscle when you wrote your PostSecret for chapter 6, but there's more where that came from. It will be hard, but share.

CHAPTER 12 | OUTCASTS

1. What is the strangest baby name you've ever heard?
2. Read Matthew 11:28-30. What does this stir up within your soul?
3. How would your life look different if you come daily to Jesus with your burdens?
4. Do you ever feel like you're the only one who struggles?
5. Where do you feel most like an outcast?
6. What will it take from you, both now and ongoing, to make your church a place of blood-stained pews?

Own Your Growth:

Who has not read this book who needs to engage in this conversation? Buy them a copy so they can join you on the journey of vulnerability.

ABOUT THE AUTHOR

Carl Kuhl is the lead pastor of Mosaic Christian Church in Elkridge, Maryland. Carl and his wife, Lindsay, planted Mosaic in 2008, and it has since been named one of the 100 fastest growing churches multiple times. His favorite thing in the world is spending time with Lindsay and their four kids.

You can reach him and get his other resources at his website carlkuhl.org.

ENDNOTES

1 "June 6, 1944." National D-Day Memorial, March 9, 2017. https://www.dday.
org/june-6-1944/#:~:text=Airborne%20Operations&text=In%20the%20
early%20hours%20of,night%20by%20over%201%2C200%20aircraft.

2 *Eagles of Mercy* (Topics Entertainment, 2015).

3 Paul Woodadge. *Angels of Mercy: Two Screaming Eagle Medics in Angoville-Au-
Plain on D-Day* (North Charleston, SC: CreateSpace Independent Publishing
Platform, 2013), 20.

4 Paul Woodage, *Eagles of Mercy: Two Screaming Eagle Medics in Angoville-
au-Plain on D-Day* (Scotts Valley, CA: CreateSpace Independent Publishing
Platform, 2013).

5 Philip Yancey, *What's So Amazing About Grace,* (Grand Rapids, MI: Zondervan,
2003), 13.

6 "Alcohol Facts and Statistics," National Institute on Alcohol Abuse and Alco-
holism (U.S. Department of Health and Human Services), accessed November
3, 2021, https://www.niaaa.nih.gov/publications/brochures-and-fact-sheets/
alcohol-facts-and-statistics.

7 Luu D. Ireland, "Who Are the 1 in 4 American Women Who Choose
Abortion?," The Conversation, May 30, 2019, https://theconversation.com/
who-are-the-1-in-4-american-women-who-choose-abortion-118016.

8 "Facts about Suicide," Centers for Disease Control and Prevention (Centers
for Disease Control and Prevention, August 30, 2021), https://www.cdc.gov/
suicide/facts/index.html.

9 "Facts & Statistics: Anxiety and Depression Association of America,
ADAA," Facts & Statistics | Anxiety and Depression Association
of America, ADAA, accessed November 3, 2021, https://adaa.org/
understanding-anxiety/facts-statistics.

10 https://www.couplestherapyinc.com/what-percentage-of-marriages-
survive-infidelity/#:~:text=Let%E2%80%99s%20Look%20at%20
the%20Stats%E2%80%A6%201%2040%25%20of,married%20to%20
their%20%E2%80%9Churt%E2%80%9D%20partners.%20More%20
items...%20

11 Chicago Tribune, "Mining 50-Year-Old Memories," baltimoresun.com (The Baltimore Sun, September 9, 2000), https://www.baltimoresun.com/news/bs-xpm-2000-09-09-0009090210-story.html.

12 Patrick Healy, "Fundamental Attribution Error: What It Is & How to Avoid It," Business Insights - Blog (Harvard Business School, June 8, 2017), https://online.hbs.edu/blog/post/the-fundamental-attribution-error?tempview=logoconvert.

13 Brené Brown, "Listening to shame," TED video, 20:22, March 2012, https://www.ted.com/talks/brene_brown_listening_to_shame?

14 Henry Cloud, *Necessary Endings: The Employees, Businesses, and Relationships That All of Us Have to Give Up in Order to Move Forward* (New York, NY: HarperCollins, 2011), 64.

15 Brown Brené, *Daring Greatly: How the Courage to Be Vulnerable Transforms the Way We Live, Love, Parent and Lead* (New York, NY: Avery, 2012).

16 Philip Yancey, *Disappointment with God: Three Questions No One Asks Aloud* (Grand Rapids, MI: Zondervan, 2015), 178–179.

17 John Ortberg, *Know Doubt: Embracing Uncertainty in Your Faith* (Grand Rapids, MI: Zondervan, 2008), 176.

18 David Van Biema, "Mother Teresa's Crisis of Faith," Time (August 23, 2007), https://time.com/4126238/mother-teresas-crisis-of-faith/

19 Ibid.

20 You can see this just in the reviews. Some believe she contradicts herself while others believe this could be one of the great books of faith, like Augustine's confessions.

21 *The Easter Experience movie*, narrated by Kyle Idleman (Louisville, KY: City On A Hill Productions, 2009), DVD.

22 Philip Yancey, *What Good Is God?* (Jericho Books, 2013).

23 I hiked this with Joel Malm and the organization he leads, Summit Leaders. I highly recommend going on a trip with Joel. You can find out more at www.summitleaders.com.

24 Mark Batterson, *Circle Maker: Praying Circles Around Your Biggest Dreams and Greatest Fears* (Grand Rapid, MI: Zondervan, 2015), 11.

25 Larry Osborne, *10 Dumb Things Smart Christians Believe* (Colorado Springs: Multnomah Books, 2009), 98.

26 E. Stanley Jones, *The Christ of the Indian Road* (New York: The Abingdon Press, 1925), 121.

27 James Emery White, *The Rise of the Nones* (Baker Book, 2014), 1.

28 John Gill, *A Complete Body of Doctrinal and Practical Divinity, Volume 3: Or, A System of Practical Tuths Deduced from the Sacred Scriptures* (London: Whittingham and Rolwand, 1796), 606.

29 "UnmissableJAPAN.com." Kintsugi – Beauty from misfortune. Accessed November 20, 2021. http://www.unmissablejapan.com/etcetera/kintsugi.

30 Casey Lesser, "The Centuries-Old Japanese Tradition of Mending Broken Ceramics with Gold," Artsy, August 24, 2018, https://www.artsy.net/article/artsy-editorial-centuries-old-japanese-tradition-mending-broken-ceramics-gold.

31 Nathaniel is protesting, post to "What is a Sabbath day's walk?", StackExchange, December 29, 2016, 7:50 p.m., https://christianity.stackexchange.com/questions/54353/what-is-a-sabbath-days-walk.

32 John Stevenson, "Sabbath Controversies," Angelfire, accessed November 15, 2021, https://www.angelfire.com/nt/theology/lk06-01.html.

33 Robert Jeffress, "What Is the Sabbath?," Pathway to Victory, June 1, 2017, https://ptv.org/devotional/what-is-the-sabbath/.

34 Rod Reynolds, "Did Jesus Break the Sabbath?," Bible Sabbath (The Bible Sabbath Association, 2005), https://www.biblesabbath.org/tss/515/sabbath.html.

35 Kim Christensen, "'Makeover' Left Her Emotionally Scarred," Los Angeles Times (Los Angeles Times, May 13, 2007), https://www.latimes.com/archives/la-xpm-2007-may-13-fi-face13-story.html.

36 Winston Churchill, "The Worst Form of Government," International Churchill Society, November 11, 1947, https://winstonchurchill.org/resources/quotes/the-worst-form-of-government/.

37 Frank Warren, *A Lifetime of Secrets: A PostSecret Book* (New York: William Morrow, 2007).

38 Philip Yancey, *Vanishing Grace: What Ever Happened to the Good News?* (London: Hodder & Stoughton, 2015).

39 AAFP, "Nearly One in 12 U.S. Adults Report Having Depression," February 2019, https://www.aafp.org/news/health-of-the-public/20180219nchsdepression.html , Johns Hopkins Medicine, "Mental Health Disorder Statistics," accessed October 2021, https://www.hopkinsmedicine.org/health/wellness-and-prevention/mental-health-disorder-statistics

40 CDC, "Illicit Drug Use", March 2021, https://www.cdc.gov/nchs/fastats/drug-use-illicit.htm

41 CDC, "Infertility," December 2019, https://www.cdc.gov/nchs/fastats/
   infertility.htm

42 https://www.nsvrc.org/statistics

43 Ibid.

44 Christopher Ingraham, "One in eight American adults is an alcoholic,
   study says," April 2019, https://www.washingtonpost.com/news/wonk/
   wp/2017/08/11/study-one-in-eight-american-adults-are-alcoholics/

45 Webroot, "Internet Pornography by the Numbers: A Significant Threat to
   Society," accessed October 2021, https://www.webroot.com/us/en/resources/
   tips-articles/internet-pornography-by-the-numbers.

46 NCDAS, "Prescription Drug Abuse Statistics," September 2021, https://
   drugabusestatistics.org/prescription-drug-abuse-statistics/

47 Frank Warren, *A Lifetime of Secrets* (William Morrow, 2007).

48 James C. Collins and Morten T. Hansen, *Great by Choice: Uncertainty, Chaos,
   and Luck: Why Some Thrive Despite Them All* (New York: HarperCollins,
   2011).

49 It sounds like a myth, but it's a legit physical condition called hematidrosis.

50 "Band of Brothers," Stephens County Georgia | Official Site, accessed
   November 15, 2021, https://stephenscountyga.gov/band-of-brothers/.

51 William Shakespeare, "Speech: 'This Day Is Called the Feast
   of...'," Poetry Foundation (Poetry Foundation), accessed November
   15, 2021, https://www.poetryfoundation.org/poems/56967/
   speech-this-day-is-called-the-feast-of-crispian.

52 Bonnie Boyle. "Bariatric Surgery, Lifestyle Interventions and Orlistat for
   Severe Obesity: The Rebalance Mixed-Methods Systematic Review and
   Economic Evaluation." Health Technology Assessment. National Institute for
   Health Research, November 4, 2021. https://www.academia.edu/61005393/
   Bariatric_surgery_lifestyle_interventions_and_orlistat_for_severe_obesity_
   the_REBALANCE_mixed_methods_systematic_review_and_economic_
   evaluation.

53 Mark Batterson, *Whisper: How to Hear the Voice of God* (Colorado Springs:
   Multnomah, 2017), 64.

54 Michael A Graham, *Cheer Up!: The Life and Ministry of Jack Miller*
   (Phillipsburg, NJ: P&R Publishing, 2020).

55 Drew Cochran, "Maryland Has Some Weird Laws, You Guys," Drew Cochran,
   Attorney at Law | Ellicott City and Annapolis, Maryland, June 19, 2017,
   https://www.drewcochranlaw.com/2017/06/19/maryland-weird-laws-guys/.

56 Steve Eighinger, "Don't Give the Family Pet a Lighted Cigar," Herald-Whig, October 20, 2020, https://www.whig.com/archive/article/dont-give-the-family-pet-a-lighted-cigar/article_962c6df2-813c-551c-bec6-035c3ced20f2.html.

57 Kelly Bayliss, "Wow! These Laws Are Stupid," NBC10 Philadelphia (NBC10 Philadelphia, March 16, 2009), https://www.nbcphiladelphia.com/local/wow-these-laws-are-stupid/2142304/.

58 "No Member of the Clergy Is Allowed to Tell Jokes or Humorous Stories from the Pulpit During a Church Service," Stupid Laws, accessed November 15, 2021, https://www.stupidlaws.com/no-member-of-the-clergy-is-allowed-to-tell-jokes-or-humorous-stories-from-the-pulpit-during-a-church-service/.

59 Paige Comstock Cunningham, "Don't Get Emotional: You Might Get Treated for Mental Illness," Salvo Magazine, 2013, https://salvomag.com/article/salvo27/dont-get-emotional.

60 Ibid.

61 C. S. Lewis, *Mere Christianity* (New York: HarperOne, 2015).

62 Paul J. Dougherty and Marlene DeMaio, "Major General Norman T. Kirk and Amputee Care During World War II," Europe PMC, June 6, 2014, https://europepmc.org/article/pmc/pmc4160475.

63 The Center for America, 15th Annual Wacky Warning Labels™ Contest: 2012 Winners Selected!, June 18, 2012, https://www.prnewswire.com/news-releases/15th-annual-wacky-warning-labels-contest-2012-winners-selected-159430055.html

64 Ibid.

65 "In Pictures: 24 Stunningly Dumb Warning Labels," Forbes (Forbes Magazine, February 23, 2011), https://www.forbes.com/2011/02/23/dumbest-warning-labels-entrepreneurs-sales-marketing-warning-labels_slide.html?sh=35c41d9c54fc.

66 Dick Winters and Cole C. Kingseed, *Beyond Band of Brothers: The War Memoirs of Major Dick Winters* (New York: Caliber, 2006).

67 Barry Schwartz, *The Paradox of Choice: Why More Is Less* (Harper Collins, 2004), 19–20.

68 John Ortberg, *If You Want to Walk on Water, You've Got to Get Out of the Boat* (Grand Rapids, MI: Zondervan, 2001), 4.

69 Frank Hurley, "The Stunning Survival Story of Ernest Shackleton and His Endurance Crew," October 2020, https://www.history.com/news/shackleton-endurance-survival

70 I use the word "legend" on purpose, as some dispute the historicity of the ad itself. The first time it appears in print seems to be in *Quit You Like Men* by Carl Hopkins Elmore in 1944.

71 Bob Russell, *When God Builds a Church: 10 Principles for Growing a Dynamic Church* (New York: Howard Books, 2010), 266.

72 Helen Shoemaker, *I Stand by the Door: The Life of Sam Shoemaker* (New York: Harper and Row, 1967).

73 Chuck Swindoll, *The Tale of the Tardy Oxcart* (Nashville, TN: Word Publishing, 1984), 214.

74 John Ortberg, *Overcoming Your Shadow Mission* (Grand Rapids, MI: Zondervan, 2008), 11.

75 Todd Hargrove, "The Said Principle," Better Movement, January 10, 2009, https://www.bettermovement.org/blog/2009/0110111.

76 "Facebook-Loving Couple Names Baby 'like,'" NBC Bay Area, May 16, 2011, https://www.nbcbayarea.com/news/local/facebook-obsessed-couple-names-baby-like/2097810/.

77 "Tu Morrow," Zimbio, accessed November 15, 2021, https://www.zimbio.com/Wacky+Celebrity+Baby+Names/articles/-h4Y8TgHt1S/Tu+Morrow.

78 Katy Gardiner, "5 Horrific Ways Bad Parents Turn Their Kids into Good Money," Cracked.com (Cracked.com, May 14, 2010), https://www.cracked.com/article_18534_5-horrific-ways-bad-parents-turn-their-kids-into-good-money.html.

79 Associated Press, "Texas Toddler at Least Third Named ESPN," ESPN (ESPN Internet Ventures, June 26, 2004), https://www.espn.com/espn/news/story?id=1829996.

80 Rachel Gillett and Samantha Lee, "60 Banned Baby Names from around the World," Business Insider (Business Insider, November 8, 2017), https://www.businessinsider.com/banned-baby-names-from-around-the-world-2016-10#france-wont-allow-a-name-if-the-courts-agree-it-will-lead-to-a-lifetime-of-mockery-1.

81 Barbara Goldberg, "New Jersey Couple Loses Custody of Son Named Adolf Hitler," ABC News (ABC News Network, August 5, 2010), https://abcnews.go.com/US/parents-cannot-regain-custody-children-nazi-inspired/story?id=11334970#:~:text=Aug.,risk%20of%20abuse%20and%20neglect.